# GROWINGPAINS

# GROWINGPAINS

## LEARNING TO LOVE MY FATHER'S FAITH

## RANDALLBALMER

Brazos Press

A Division of Baker Book House Co
Grand Rapids, Michigan 49516

Published by Brazos Press
a division of Baker Book House Company
P.O. Box 6287, Grand Rapids, MI 49516-6287

Printed in the United States of America

Scripture marked as RSV is taken from the Revised Standard Version of the Bible, copyright 1946, 1952, 1971 by the Division of Christian Education of the National Council of the Churches of Christ in the USA. Used by permission.

Scripture marked as NASB is taken from the NEW AMERICAN STANDARD BIBLE®. Copyright © The Lockman Foundation 1960, 1962, 1963, 1968, 1971, 1972, 1973, 1975, 1977, 1995. Used by permission.

Scripture marked as NKJV is taken from the New King James Version. Copyright © 1979, 1980, 1982 by Thomas Nelson, Inc. Used by permission. All rights reserved.

"Cat's in the Cradle" by Harry Chapin and Sandy Chapin © Story Songs, Ltd. All rights administered by W B Music Corp. All rights reserved. Used by Permission of Warner Bros. Publications U.S. Inc., Miami, Fl. 33014.

**Library of Congress Cataloging-in-Publication Data**

Balmer, Randall Herbert.
    Growing pains : learning to love my father's faith / Randall Balmer.
        p.   cm.
    ISBN 1-58743-018-5 (cloth)
    1. Balmer, Randall Herbert. 2. Christian biography—United States. I. Title.

BR1725.B333 A3 2001
277.3'0825'092—dc21
[B]                                          2001035456

For current information about all releases from Brazos Press, visit our web site:
http://www.brazospress.com

Also by Randall Balmer

*Religion in Twentieth Century America*
*Blessed Assurance: A History of Evangelicalism in America*
*Grant Us Courage: Travels Along the Mainline of American Protestantism*
*The Presbyterians* (co-written with John R. Fitzmier)
*Mine Eyes Have Seen the Glory: A Journey into the Evangelical Subculture in*
    *America*
*A Perfect Babel of Confusion: Dutch Religion and English Culture*
    *in the Middle Colonies*

for Clarence R. Balmer
(1929–1997)
son, brother, husband, father, grandfather
and minister of the gospel

*'til we meet at Jesus' feet*

# CONTENTS

## PART 3    GLIMPSES OF GRACE

To really want the truth, to long for it desperately, is to reject every formulation and theory and dogma and opinion right up to the time you see and touch and unite with the Being or Thing itself! Nobody ever discovers truth by barfing up sunday-school answers to questions.

DAVID JAMES DUNCAN

I know nothing, except what everyone knows—if there when Grace dances, I should dance.

W. H. AUDEN

. . . when I grew up I found that life handed you these rusty bent old tools—friendships, prayer, conscience, honesty—and said, Do the best you can with these, they will have to do. And mostly, against all odds, they're enough.

ANNE LAMOTT

Holy Jesu, grant us tears.

I. WILLIAMS

Any God I ever felt in church I brought with me. And I think all the other folks did too. They came to church to share God, not find God.

ALICE WALKER

# PREFACE

Des Moines, Iowa
August 14, 1997

I t's the kind of day you dreamed about during those last years of exile on the Left Coast. A breeze gently purls the crops and the prairie grasses. The sky is blue and endless and endlessly blue. It almost pierces the eyes.

Summer is everywhere. You'll be happy to know that the farmers have plenty of rain this year, and so the loamy earth gives off a faint, musty scent—the promise of a copious harvest, the smell of heaven. Already, the woman down the road is selling sweet corn from the back of her pickup truck. Out here, beyond the edge of town, a score of blackbirds congregates briefly on the telephone wire and then disperses. A lone mourning dove calls from the fencepost.

Mom is doing pretty well, I think. She still struggles with pronouns. *We*—and then a hasty correction: *I. Our*, then *my*. "I have my moments," she says, "and it's still hard to climb into that empty bed at night." But she soldiers on. I suppose that if rearing five complicated sons doesn't instill resilience, nothing will.

11

She's planted a small garden in back of the house. It looks rather helpless and pathetic by your standards, but you'd be proud of her. "Every time I come out here to pull a few weeds," she told me this morning, "I say, 'Sorry, Dad.'" I think she knows how much you would have loved just one more summer scratching at the soil and then plopping the harvest triumphantly on the kitchen counter— fists full of cucumbers and radishes and carrots and beets and sweet corn and *real* tomatoes. Then you'd disappear, scrub the soil from beneath your fingernails, and sit down to the taste of summer.

One more garden. One last summer to spend romping with the grandkids.

I've decided to set down a few thoughts. On the face of it these reflections are about you and me and the lover's quarrel we sustained for the better part of three decades over matters of faith and belief and piety—and politics and parenting and whatever else we could find to disagree about. At another level, I think they speak to larger, more general issues of faith, for I have come to believe that, although faith is a gift, it must be seized boldly.

I think you taught me that. The pages that follow are full of things you taught me, although I usually learned them by resistance and struggle and finally a kind of grudging appropriation. Not that you won every argument. I still resist and struggle and push against everything you taught me.

As I look over these words I see a lot of anger and resentment, but I also see movement and (if I may say so) some maturation. I was tempted, I confess, to file off some of the rough edges in the early pieces, to modulate the tone a bit, but I decided to keep them pretty much as they were written (or preached or spoken) because they capture changes over time. Embedded somewhere in these pages, I think, is a larger narrative about estrangement and love, despair and hope, sin and grace, alienation and reconciliation.

And fathers and sons. As a parent of teenagers now myself, I appreciate as I couldn't before the challenge of passing the faith from one generation to the next. I recognize the anxiety you must have faced as five sons navigated the troubled waters of adolescence, intent on their rebellions. But we came through it, I think, all of us— and each in his own way. That may be, I see now, your crowning achievement in a lifetime of remarkable success: seeing your sons safely to Jesus (perhaps *that* is what we should have inscribed on your tombstone). Even though I was the eldest—perhaps *because* I was the eldest—I'm afraid that my journey was longer and more torturous than my brothers'.

Mom has a rhubarb pie in the oven—our old favorite recipe, yours and mine—and she's plucked a few tomatoes from the garden. Out here, on the edge of town, the shadows from the oak tree are getting longer, and the mourning dove repeats its plaintive call from the fencepost. The breeze has faded a bit as we edge toward sunset, but it still carries the scent of heaven.

I'd better be heading back now. It's supper time.

# PART 1

# FATHER, HEAR MY CRY

Out of the depths I cry to thee
O Father, hear me calling.
Incline thine ear to my distress
In spite of my rebelling.

MARTIN LUTHER

# FAITH OF OUR FATHERS

Hear, O LORD, when I cry aloud, be gracious to me and answer me! Thou hast said, "Seek ye my face." My heart says to thee, "Thy face, LORD, do I seek." Hide not thy face from me. Turn not thy servant away in anger, thou who hast been my help. Cast me not off, forsake me not, O God of my salvation! For my father and my mother have forsaken me, but the LORD will take me up.

PSALM 27:7–10 (RSV)

On my desk in New York sits a photograph of a seven-year-old boy. He's wearing a pair of glasses, a freshly ironed shirt buttoned to the neck, and his best smile. I placed that picture on my desk at the suggestion of a friend who understood that, as someone who grew up fundamentalist, I was having a difficult time finding my way as an adult. Just look at that picture of yourself as a child, he suggested, and try to recall what it was like to be that child.

For weeks, the only response that picture inspired in me was laughter. The photograph was taken in 1961, and all my hair was chopped off. That, combined with the spectacles perched awkwardly on my nose, made for a comic figure.

But then one morning, while seated at my desk, it all came back. In 1961, we lived in a parsonage next to the church out in the farm country of southern Minnesota, and there was nothing in the world more important to me than baseball. One day my father returned from town with a plastic bat and ball. "Let's play ball," he said. I couldn't have been more excited, in part because I knew, even then, that my father had no interest whatsoever in sports of any kind. I recall what happened next as though it were yesterday. After swinging wildly at a couple of pitches, I decided to let a few go by. Somehow, even in first grade, I had learned enough about baseball to know that four balls constituted a walk and, perhaps to save myself the embarrassment of swinging and missing more pitches, I elected to draw a base on balls.

"Well, what's the point of all this?" my father huffed. "If you don't swing I'm just wasting my time." He tossed the ball in my direction, turned, and headed back to his study.

We never played ball again.

I tell that story not to elicit sympathy and certainly not to suggest that my father acted out of malice, for I realize now that he brought his own brokenness to his role as parent. Yet it would be difficult to overestimate the loneliness and abandonment felt by the kid in glasses. I relate that story because, just a bit more than halfway through my allotted three-score-and-ten years, I have come to believe that we, all of us in the community of faith, have stories to tell. "We are healed by our stories," Terry Tempest Williams declares. And perhaps, through luck or coincidence or even grace, my story might help you understand your story.

As I stared at the picture on my desktop and remembered that breezy Minnesota afternoon, I began to realize that, throughout my life, my perception of God was very much tied to my childish perception of my father—distant and austere, disapproving and abandoning. Psychologists call this conditional love. I will love you, provided that you meet my conditions. And if you fail at any time to live up to my expectations, I will withhold that love.

In the midst of my tears that morning in my office I recognized that I had spent most of my life hoping that my father would pitch to me again. There I was, a gawky kid in glasses and a crewcut, standing in the middle of the Minnesota prairie with a new baseball bat slumped over his shoulder, waiting to play ball. Maybe, just maybe, if this kid smiled harder, if he excelled in school, if he suffered through piano lessons, if he obeyed all the rules, or if he memorized enough Bible verses, his father would emerge from his study to hit a few grounders or to pitch a few more. This time, he vowed, he would swing at every pitch.

As this kid moved from childhood to adolescence, he continued to work hard to win the approval of his father—getting good grades in school, becoming president of the youth group at church, attending an evangelical college, and marrying a "good Christian girl." Then, later, on to seminary and graduate school, an appointment at an Ivy League university, tenure, and a string of professional successes.

But something, somewhere, went wrong, although I tried to ignore it for a long time. Why did my life seem empty, despite all of my achievements? Why did I find going to church such utter drudgery? Why was my Bible gathering dust on the bookshelf? Why did God— this same God I had celebrated for years in Sunday school as "closer than a brother"—why did that God seem so remote and distant? What happened to the triumphant Christian life that I was supposed to experience, moving from victory to victory until I tasted sweet union with Jesus?

For a long time I despaired of answering those questions. That "happiness in Jesus" was so elusive that I gave up the quest. For the better part of a decade I tried to put my childhood and my fundamentalist past behind me, not so much out of rebellion as out of personal dissatisfaction. The evangelical faith of my parents simply wasn't living up to its billing. "Victory in Jesus" remained beyond my grasp. God was preoccupied and elusive, and when I called on him for guidance or comfort or solace, as I did often, he couldn't be bothered; he was, no doubt, working on a sermon for next Sunday.

Why was I having such difficulty sustaining my faith? Why was I so indifferent toward God? Some time ago, deep in the midst of a personal crisis, I visited Doug, an old friend on the West Coast, someone who, like me, had grown up fundamentalist. He pointed out that many evangelicals, including the leaders of evangelicalism, projected their views of their fathers onto God. Many of the spokesmen for postwar evangelicalism, for example, had been abandoned, either physically or emotionally, by their fathers. The evangelical God they wrote and talked about, Doug suggested, was an austere God of judgment, a stern and demanding father rather than a gentle and compassionate friend.

This made sense to me. I recalled some of the prayers I had heard in church through the years—"O Father, come and be among us; let us feel your presence"—and I began to wonder if I wasn't hearing the anguished cry of a son searching for his daddy. Why did evangelicals impose so many rules and strictures on themselves and on their children? Perhaps it had something to do with the way they viewed God—as a parent, judgmental and demanding, always keeping a tally of our shortcomings and prepared to withhold his approval, his love, from anyone who fell short of the standards. The book of Genesis tells us that God created humanity in God's own image, but it seemed that we fundamentalists had done the opposite: We had created God in our image or, more precisely, in the image of our fathers. We had concocted this deity whose love was conditioned on our behaving in certain ways. This God was distant and disapproving. This God's love was conditional.

As Doug and I talked about this God we decided that he (and I use the male pronoun advisedly) was not very attractive. This was a God who, like our fathers, demanded perfection. If we hoped to gain entry into heaven, we had better toe the line, otherwise we could expect utter abandonment, consignment to hell. This God of our projections was not a God who gave us permission to embrace life in all of its ambiguity and complexity, let alone to embrace ourselves in all of our ambiguity and complexity. This, in fact, was a God who refused to recognize ambiguity altogether, who forced us to see the world in dualistic categories—good and bad, black and white, right and wrong—with no allowance whatsoever for anything in between. This God, just like the evangelicals who invented him, viewed the Christian life as a steady ascent toward holiness. Once you had been born again, once you had "prayed the prayer," you could expect to move onward and upward in your faith, and if that trajectory didn't hold, if you faltered along the way, well, you were doing something wrong.

As Doug and I regarded each other on that chilly morning in November, we both knew that something was very wrong. The triumphant Christian life that evangelicals talked about couldn't have been more alien to us. Both of us had been neglected by fathers who were too busy doing the Lord's work. We had been beaten and battered by life. We had betrayed those who loved us, and we had been spurned by those we loved. We were riddled with guilt. So many times each of us had felt lonely and abandoned, and the faith of our fathers offered precious little comfort. We had known grief and sorrow, and we found a camaraderie in our suffering.

At that terrifying moment in my life, perched on the edge of hopelessness and despair, Doug looked me in the eye, for he is a true friend, and he saw into my soul. With the wisdom and compassion of a fellow pilgrim, he suggested that I consider anew the good news of the New Testament. Coming from him, this advice, I knew, was not empty piety. Jesus, after all, had come into the world not to anoint the saints but to save that which was lost. Jesus, having tasted of our humanity, understood our suffering. He of all people knew that what we now so blithely call the Christian life was not some kind of cosmic victory lap.

Doug encouraged me to take seriously the ancient Christian teaching that, in Jesus, God became man, and suggested that if I wanted a truer picture of God, I had to set aside, at least for the moment, my notions of God as father, with all of the psychological baggage that implies, and consider God the son, Jesus.

Some time later, I began to catch a glimpse of this Jesus. I was sitting in church just before Christmas when suddenly the sermon faded to black, I turned my head upward, and in some intuitive way that I cannot explain, I saw Jesus. Not the Sunday school Jesus I thought I knew and found I didn't like very much, but a Jesus of compassion, the man of sorrows acquainted with grief. This is the Jesus who wandered in the wilderness for forty days and forty nights. This is the Jesus who was betrayed by his friends. This is the Jesus who embodied the abandonment of all humanity, who while hanging on the cross, suspended between heaven and earth with his arms outstretched, cried out in despair and sadness and utter abandonment, *"Eloi, Eloi, lama sabachthani,"* which is to say, "My God, my God! Why have you forsaken me?"

And if I can translate those words yet again, I hear the anguished voice of a distraught son. "Daddy? Daddy! Where are you, Daddy?"

As I sat in church that wintry December morning I saw the *humanity* of Jesus for the first time. I saw him during his moment on the cross not as the Son of God proclaiming victory over sin but as the Son of Man, alone and abandoned, at the end of his rope. I identified with Jesus in his moment of utter despair and hopelessness.

But many Christians, Protestants especially, are uncomfortable with this vision of God, a God who, in Jesus, somehow reflects the alienation of all humanity—alienation from God, from one another, from ourselves, from our fathers. How many sermons have we heard about the *empty* cross, signifying the resurrection and triumph over sin, rather than Jesus *on the cross,* as in Roman Catholic iconography? We like victory. We prefer winners, a God who has conquered, which, as the feminists remind us, is a very masculine view of God, a kind of marauding deity who vanquishes evil and doubt and darkness. The Almighty as Chuck Norris or Arnold Schwarzenegger. We like this triumphant God because we too fancy ourselves conquerors, marching from victory to victory. We don't like the idea of God hanging on the cross. It suggests travail and suffering and defeat, and it makes us uncomfortable.

I confess that I no longer find much in common with traditional Protestant conceptions of God the Father, with God as the conquering hero. There are not many days when I feel like a conqueror. More often, at least at this juncture of my life, I feel broken and alone and abandoned, and in those moments I feel solace from Jesus on the cross, because he too was broken and alone and abandoned.

I know that in some profound and intuitive way I feel connected to this Jesus on the cross. I identify with him, with his abandonment, his loneliness, his alienation. I can even say that I love him, not because, in the unfortunate words of that Sunday school ditty, he first loved me, because that suggests duty or obligation. I love him because I see in him the abandoned child, the suffering servant, the man of sorrows acquainted with grief, and I know that, though I walk through the valley of the shadow of death, my travails pale before his.

This is the God of liberation, not judgment, of hope in the face of despair. This God, who took on human form, allows me to embrace my own humanity.

How does all this relate to the child in glasses, the one whose picture sits on my desk in New York? I no longer laugh when I look at him, for I can now see beyond the spectacles and into his eyes. I see his innocence and his vulnerability. I see how desperately he wants to be loved. I see how hard he tries to win the approval of those around him. I see him in Sunday school singing, "Jesus loves me, this I know, for the Bible tells me so." And I know that seven-year-old boy has no idea, as he belts out the melody at the top of his lungs, how much he will come to rely on the profound truth of those simple words three and four decades later.

The kid in glasses still loves baseball. Every year at the beginning of spring training he still half expects a telegram from the Detroit Tigers. It would read something like this:

DEAR MR BALMER STOP WE'VE MADE
A TERRIBLE MISTAKE STOP HAVE AN
OPENING AT SECOND BASE THIS
SEASON AND THINK YOU STILL HAVE
A COUPLE OF GOOD YEARS LEFT IN
YOU STOP PLEASE REPORT TO THE
TRAINING FACILITY IN LAKELAND
IMMEDIATELY

I passed yet another February without receiving my telegram, and I think that, closing in on my forty-somethingth birthday, I may soon be grown up enough to recognize that I will never make it to the major leagues. But I have more confidence about my pilgrimage toward God. I have come to see the Christian life no longer as a steep and steady ascent toward holiness but as a tortuous journey full of twists and turns and switchbacks and perhaps a rockslide or two along the way.

But in the course of that journey I feel the embrace of a God who accepts me as I am in all of my humanity, who loves me unconditionally, in spite of my shortcomings. It is a pilgrimage of joy and sadness, of loving and suffering, triumph and tragedy, but it culminates in sweet union with Jesus, who somehow takes our sad and broken lives and makes us whole. That's the gospel, I think. That sounds like good news to me.

And at that moment of wholeness, perhaps I can persuade Jesus, this man of sorrows acquainted with grief, to hit me a few grounders.

# THE GENERATION OF FAITH

And Jacob was left alone; and a man wrestled with him until the breaking of the day. When the man saw that he did not prevail against Jacob, he touched the hollow of his thigh; and Jacob's thigh was put out of joint as he wrestled with him. Then [the man] said, "Let me go, for the day is breaking." But Jacob said, "I will not let you go, unless you bless me." And he said to him, "What is your name?" And he said, "Jacob." Then he said, "Your name shall no more be called Jacob, but Israel, for you have striven with God and with men, and have prevailed." Then Jacob asked him, "Tell me, I pray, your name." But he said, "Why is it that you ask my name?" And there he blessed him. So Jacob called the name of the place Peniel, saying, "For I have seen God face to face, and yet my life is preserved." The sun rose upon him as he passed Peniel, limping because of his thigh.

GENESIS 32:24–31 (RSV)

envied them in a way—their ease and self-confidence, the way they glided smartly across campus, their new American Tourister briefcases in tow. Moving from class to class, they knew—almost instinctively, it seemed—when to laugh at the professor's remarks. They asked all the right questions; they learned all the right answers. They were clean cut and well groomed and athletic and earnest and attentive. They smiled most of the time. They socialized effortlessly among themselves, guffawing at inside jokes. More than anything else, they exuded an air of confidence and self-assurance.

These were men of God, studying for the ministry at a fundamentalist seminary, and I was supposed to be among them. For as long as I can remember I had been groomed for the ministry, which is to say that my devout parents expected great things of me. My Christmas present following my fifth birthday was a three-foot-high replica of my father's pulpit, and family lore abounds with recollections of me as a five-year-old stemwinding preacher. I sang "Jesus loves me, this I know" in Sunday school, and "The B-I-B-L-E, yes, that's the book for me" and "Jesus wants me for a sunbeam."

I was "saved" at the age of three at the kitchen table in the back of a parsonage overlooking the Minnesota prairie. After breakfast and our family devotions, my father asked if I was ready to invite Jesus into my heart. For some reason, I have a vivid mental image of the toaster, its brown fabric-covered cord trailing off the table. Yes, of course I would renounce my sinfulness and ask Jesus into my heart, and from that moment on I was saved. I had been born again.

I grew up in the secure cocoon of fundamentalist faith, society, and dogma. I was a quick study and learned from an early age to detect who was saved and who wasn't. The Lutherans up the road were a bit suspect, what with all their vestments and dead liturgy. Baptists were pretty much okay, though God knows they could get cantankerous at times. Roman Catholics, of course, were beyond the pale. I knew, for example, that I could never pursue the crush I had on Mary Kay Zimmer at school because she was Catholic, and my parents had informed me gently, but in no uncertain terms, that if I married anyone other than a *Christian* girl I would be disowned.

There were, I soon learned, other ways to tell who was saved and who wasn't. Smokers were non-Christians because they defiled their bodies, and our body was a temple of the Lord. Drinking was also a sign of wickedness, and when my dad served Holy Communion at church it was grape juice, not wine, and it came in tiny glass containers barely larger than a thimble. Dancing was also a sign of "worldliness." The "Apostle Paul"—for a while I thought "Apostle" was his first name; we couldn't say "Saint Paul" because that was too Catholic—had admonished us to be separate from the world, to be *in* the world but not *of* the world. As Christians, we were called out of the world; our real citizenship lay in heaven, not on this earth, and this world, after all, was doomed and transitory. Jesus was coming back at any moment, and we had better be ready. Don't let Jesus catch you on the dance floor or in a movie theater.

I learned my lessons well. Rarely did I slip my fundamentalist moorings, and when I did I stayed pretty close to shore, even during the perilous years of adolescence. I shuffled off to Bible camp in the summer, where I swam and hiked and braided lanyards and fell in love and rededicated my life to Jesus at the campfire a couple of dozen times.

What's it like to grow up fundamentalist? I hear that question a lot, especially from friends in New York, along with the corollaries: Is it true your parents didn't let you play cards? Did you really have to bring a note excusing you from square dancing in gym class? Your parents made you go to church more than once a week? What about sex? No sex before marriage, really?

I've always detected an undercurrent of voyeurism in these questions, but, for the record, the answer is yes to all of the above. No cards, no dancing, church three or four days a week and at least twice on Sunday. And no premarital sex. I had to sneak off to my first motion picture at the age of sixteen, feeling dreadfully guilty the whole time. We didn't have a television until I was nearly ten, although I'm not sure if that was because of religious conviction or relative poverty. Probably a bit of both.

Growing up fundamentalist meant living in a tiny world where every question had an answer. It was a world inebriated with rhetoric about authority and obsessed with chains of command—the authority of the Bible, the authority of the church, the pastor, the husband, the father—and all of it dominated by authoritarian preachers, too many of them sporting egos roughly the size of Montana.

It was a world marked by pious rhetoric, a kind of cloying God-talk. "Did you get that promotion? Well, praise the Lord!" "My heart was really challenged by that message." "God has been so good to me; I don't deserve his favors." "The Lord has given me a real heart for the unsaved." "I just wanna do God's will."

There was comfort in that world, I'll not deny it. There's a certain appeal to being cosseted in a subculture with little room for ambiguity, where my destiny, both heavenly and earthly, had already been determined. Yet here I was watching these seminarians armed with their briefcases and their self-assurance. They had stuck with the program. They had solved the riddle of faith, which for them was really no riddle at all. Ask them a question, any question, and they could supply you with an answer. They could recite the cosmological and the ontological arguments backward and forward, along with an airtight case for biblical inerrancy, the virgin birth, and the premillennial return of Jesus. Belief for them was effortless and easy, and I envied them. Yes, I envied them.

I was twenty-two at the time, a year out of college, and unemployed. After extensive deliberation I had turned down a career as an underwriter for Allstate Insurance Company, and as I looked for gainful employment I knew I was searching for something else: I was searching for the certainty I saw on the scrubbed faces of the seminarians. I knew I hadn't become the sunbeam Jesus apparently wanted. In the argot of the evangelical subculture, I was "willful" and "wayward"; I had slipped my moorings and was drifting in doubt and uncertainty.

A kind of intellectual restlessness had overtaken me. I was enamored of the world of ideas, so for a time I thought the way to reclaim the faith lay in rational argumentation, intellectual respectability. I was embarrassed by the simple piety of my parents, so I tried to dress up evangelical convictions in Enlightenment finery. Phrases like "reasoned belief" and the "integration of faith and learning" tripped off my tongue and became a kind of mantra. The theological discipline of apologetics seemed like the right course. If only we fundamentalists could come up with a reasonable defense of the faith, then we could hold our heads high in the marketplace of ideas. More important, we could distance ourselves from those loopy charismatics and pentecostals, who gave us all a bad name with their naive reliance on religious experience.

Attending church at that juncture of my life was excruciating, so painful that I rarely tried. The sentiments I acknowledged at the time were anger and betrayal, but the subculture still had enough of a hold on me that I felt embarrassed as well, ashamed that the faith had not taken hold of me—or had I not taken hold of the faith?—the way I thought it should. When guilt overtook me and I did show up at church, I heard vapid and self-congratulatory sermons about the goodness of God and the rewards of living a "good Christian life." I heard admonitions about avoiding the perils of worldliness and triumphal assurances that God would eventually vanquish his adversaries, if not in this world then assuredly in the next. This God struck me as austere and demanding; he seemed to be big on rules, to hear the preachers tell it.

After a couple of decades steeped in fundamentalism, I found the whole business rather nauseating—the megalomaniacal preachers, the cloying God-talk, the overweening moralism—and so I trotted off to graduate school and immersed myself further in the life of the mind. Fundamentalism, with its petty squabbles over doctrinal minutiae and its taboos about beer and hair length and motion pictures,

29

couldn't have been farther from my consciousness. I was busy building a career of my own, and I couldn't care less about the smug seminarians with their self-righteous patter about God's will and sanctification and all their hoary theological schemes.

Despite my satisfaction with the life of the mind, however, the life of the Spirit still beckoned, and I count this as a remarkable working of grace. Shortly after settling into my first academic appointment, I decided, in effect, to revisit my past, although I didn't recognize that I was doing so at the time. I set out on a journey into the evangelical subculture in America with the idea of lending some perspective to the televangelist scandals then titillating the media in the mid-1980s. I visited churches and camp meetings and seminaries and Bible camps. I heard plenty of bad sermons in the course of my travels and more renditions of "Shine, Jesus, Shine" than I care to count, but I also started hearing the gospel. I heard the gospel in the strains of "Amazing Grace, How Sweet the Sound" and in the simple expressions of piety of folks with their arms upraised to Jesus. I heard the gospel in an old friend's lament that fundamentalists had taken the gracious, beckoning words of Jesus and twisted them into demands, threats, and moral imperatives.

I don't think I heard much of the gospel during my visit to a fundamentalist Bible camp in the Adirondack Mountains of upstate New York, but there, as the flames of the campfire licked the darkness, my life began to make sense to me. I saw how desperately my parents wanted to rear me in the faith, how they wanted me to have the same conversion to fundamentalist Christianity that had so profoundly shaped their own lives. At the same time, however, as I listened to teenagers around the campfire talk about their own spiritual lives, I saw how difficult it was for me to appropriate my parents' faith. They had socialized me in the church since infancy—Sunday school, sermons, family devotions, Bible camp—and yet they expected that my moment of conversion would have the same transformative power as theirs. That, I concluded, was unrealistic because my "conversion"

30

at age three was, at best, a ratification of the beliefs and the regimen that had been drilled into me since birth.

I saw myself in the adolescent faces around the campfire that night. I recognized the urge, under the extraordinary pressure of parents and peers, to give my life to Jesus, to conjure the right religious emotions, and then to declare my readiness to live a "good Christian life" and abide by all the fundamentalist strictures. I also recognized myself in those who, choking back tears, were "rededicating" their lives to Jesus, those whose conversions hadn't generated the emotion or the transformation they thought was expected of them, so they were revisiting the moment, this time "rededicating" their lives to Jesus as the flames danced and the embers glowed.

My experience at the Bible camp prompted me to reconsider my own struggle with faith. With the encouragement of a fellow pilgrim, I discarded my image of the self-confident seminarians and the triumphalist preachers. I even set aside the imposing specter of God the Father, who had been portrayed to me as demanding and authoritarian. I found Jesus a much more sympathetic figure. Jesus, I suspected, wouldn't have felt very comfortable with the briefcase crowd either. As nearly as I could tell, he hung around with ne'er-do-wells, people on the margins of society—fishermen and tax collectors and adulterers and lepers.

In time, it occurred to me that the entire Bible was populated with scoundrels. Paul certainly fits that description, both before and after his conversion. Peter didn't score too well on the loyalty test. David could not have become a member of any fundamentalist church that I'm aware of; he was hardly the poster boy for "traditional family values."

And yet the Bible seems to celebrate these characters. God chooses Paul—irascible old Paul, who had graduated at the top of his class at the persecution academy, to be the conduit for spreading the gospel. Jesus surely must have given Peter his nickname, The Rock, with his tongue at least partially in cheek, to call attention to

31

the fact that, with his spineless dithering, Peter was anything but solid. David, the Scriptures tell us, was a man after God's own heart.

Then there's Jacob, dear Jacob. He heads the list of scoundrels. Jacob, you'll recall, was the guy who, disguised beneath a goatskin, cadges his brother's rightful inheritance while Esau is out fetching supper. Jacob gets his comeuppance a bit when, after working seven years for the woman he loves, his devious father-in-law delivers the wrong woman to Jacob's marriage bed. Jacob works another seven years and finally secures Rachel for his second wife. He succeeds pretty well in the ranching business and then one day, camped out in the hill country, word arrives that Esau and his entourage are about to drop by. Jacob, all alone and sweating bullets, finally beds down by the Jabbok River and, in the course of a fitful night, grapples with a phantom—a man or an angel, perhaps, or even God—a wrestling match that leaves him with a bum leg.

Whatever else you care to say about these characters, they strike me as quintessentially human—Jacob and Paul and David and Peter and a hundred others whose images flicker before us in the Bible, however briefly. They are three-dimensional beings with a substance to them that I found lacking in the role models of my fundamentalist past. The religion of my childhood, not to mention the seminarians who so unnerved me, had taken the stories of these wonderfully complex and textured characters and reduced them to morality plays—abject sinners who suddenly are transformed into good, rule-abiding Christians.

Through some unaccountable working of grace, I began to see them not so much as saints but as fellow pilgrims. Like me, they are flawed. They trudge along, step by step, just like most of us mortals. What they share in common, I think, is a sense that the call of God is the call to be human, to embrace our humanity in all of its ambiguity. They see that the call of God is a summons to embark upon a journey of faith whose destiny is not always apparent. The Book of Hebrews tells us that when Abraham, another character with a checkered past, answered the call of God, "he went out, not knowing where he was to go" (Heb. 11:8 RSV).

In David James Duncan's novel *The River Why*, Gus Orviston, the central character, is a maniacal fisherman (like those first followers of Jesus) who unwittingly finds himself on a spiritual quest. After hours of debate and conversation, Gus's spiritual adviser, an aspiring fisherman himself, finally cuts to the chase. "I'm not sane, Gus. I believe in the rivers of living water; I believe our souls swim in that water; I believe Jesus and Buddha and Krishna are the savour in that water; I believe in the Garden World and its Queen. I love the ol' Whopper."

The path of faith is not tidy. For many, belief itself is an affront to intelligence and even to sanity, especially when you can explain the spiritual quest in psychological or sociological or physiological terms. But, like Gus Orviston's interlocutor, like Paul and David, I believe in the rivers of living water, and those rivers sustain me in my pilgrimage. For me, the path to faith has been rocky and my steps uneven. I am plagued by doubts and fears and anxieties. I feel desolate, at times, and my cries to God meet with silence. I have been locked in a lovers' quarrel with my father, the preacher, for the better part of three decades, a quarrel over faith and belief and theology that has not so much abated as it has taken a different form since his passing. Like Abraham, I'm not always certain where I'm going on this pilgrimage, and my progress is slowed, I'm sure, whenever I pause to wrestle with God—or someone—lurking there in the darkness. My trajectory is rarely straight and not always upward. It resembles, at times, the woven, brown cord of a toaster trailing off the table. . . .

And yet, what sustains me is a sense, or at least the hope, of divine presence, that I am not alone on this pilgrimage, but I am in the company of friends who will pick me up from time to time, dust me off, and point me in the right direction. What sustains me is a suspicion that there is still enchantment in the world—in the air on top of a mountain, in the crunch of leaves beneath a harvest moon,

33

in the dazzling colors on the flanks of a rainbow trout, in the sound of wind brushing past pine needles. What sustains me is the laughter of my sons. What sustains me is the delight of love and companionship and making love. What sustains me is the conviction that the journey brings its own rewards, regardless of the destination, that holiness is somehow imbedded in the process itself.

I believe because of the epiphanies, small and large, that have intersected my path—small, discrete moments of grace when I have sensed a kind of superintending presence outside of myself. I believe because these moments—a kind word, an insight, an anthem on Easter morning, a chill in the spine—are too precious to discard, and I choose not to trivialize them by reducing them to rational explanation. I believe because, for me, the alternative to belief is far too daunting. I believe because, at the turn of the twenty-first century, belief itself is an act of defiance in a society still enthralled by the blandishments of Enlightenment rationalism.

I no longer envy the seminarians I knew twenty years ago, even though I'm sure those spiritual athletes are far ahead of me on the journey. I congratulate them on their self-confidence. They figured out all of their answers before I even knew the questions, and I will never be able to match their strides.

Perhaps you, too, are a pilgrim, and if you look for me, check somewhere toward the back of the pack. Like Jacob, I'm the guy with a limp.

# CHRISTIAN PIETY
# THROUGH THE GENERATIONS

"Only take heed, and keep your soul diligently, lest you forget
the things which your eyes have seen, and lest they depart
from your heart all the days of your life; make them known to
your children and your children's children—how on the day
that you stood before the LORD your God at Horeb, the LORD
said to me, 'Gather the people to me, that I may let them hear
my words, so that they may learn to fear me all the days that
they live upon the earth, and that they may teach their children so.'"

DEUTERONOMY 4:9–10 (RSV)

R eferring to Gilbert Tennent, the eighteenth-century Presby-
terian revivalist, John Loring reported to his father in 1740 that
"Mr Tennant went out of Town on Monday to Charlestown. . . .
On Sabbath day he preached in the afternoon for Mr Cooper and
in the evening at our meeting from those words, how shall we escape
if we neglect so great Salvation. I hope I shall think of that text often

and by that means make my flight to Jesus by faith and lay hold of him and not let him go till he has blest me."

Something about this letter struck me when I ran across it at the Massachusetts Historical Society some time ago. The earnestness of this young correspondent captured my imagination, especially when I learned that he was writing to his father, Israel Loring, a Puritan minister.

As I continued reading through those dusty files, I began to pick up a thread of correspondence between John Loring and his father. The younger Loring would regularly report on the progress of the revival then convulsing the Atlantic colonies, and then he would add a note of hope that his own heart would eventually be moved by the gospel. Consider, for instance, his letter of January 22, 1741: "I trust God will make me willing in the day of his power. I hope Sir you will not be unmindfull of me at the throne of grace. O that my stony heart might be taken from me and that god would give me a heart of flesh that I might Serve him in newness of life and new obedience so that old things might pass away and all things become new within me. Sir let that be your petition for me and whilst you are thus doing for me I hope I shall be enabled to do so too in sincerity & uprightness of heart."

Over the last several years, I have become intrigued by what I call the generational problem in religion: How do you pass the faith from one generation to the next? Indeed, the Puritans of New England faced real difficulties. When it came time in the seventeenth century to transfer the mantle of leadership to the second generation, that generation found itself unworthy. How could they, after all, measure up to the spiritual standards of their mothers and fathers? The founding generation of New England had sacrificed fortune and family in the Old World, made a perilous ocean crossing, and proceeded to carve a godly society out of the howling wilderness of Massachusetts. When it was the children's turn to stand in front of the meetinghouse to give account of their own spiritual experiences, they found it difficult, indeed impossible, to do so because their piety and devotion paled so abjectly next to that of their parents.

Chaim Potok's novel *The Chosen* takes up the same issue in another religious context. Reb Saunders, a Hasidic rebbe in Brooklyn, desperately wants his son Danny to succeed him as leader of his Hasidic congregation. Danny, a precocious child, can cite long passages of the Jewish Scriptures from memory. He dumbfounds his father and members of his father's congregation with his command of even the most recondite passages of the Talmud. But he cannot summon the requisite piety, and so he bids his father an anguished farewell and, shorn of his earlocks, walks off into a new life.

Other groups and individuals in American history have faced the same problem. I've already mentioned John Loring of eighteenth-century Boston. Catharine Beecher, daughter of Lyman Beecher, struggled all of her life to live up to the piety and reputation of her redoubtable father. Evangelicals wrestle over this generational problem, as do the Amish and the Mennonites and even, I dare say, a few Methodists and Presbyterians.

This issue of generational piety seems to be lurking behind the text in Deuteronomy. Moses, forbidden by God to cross the Jordan into the promised land because of his disobedience, delivers a kind of valedictory speech to the Israelites. Go in and take the land, Moses declares, with, no doubt, a tinge of remorse that he can only gaze at it from across the river. "Keep the commandments of the LORD your God . . . and keep your soul diligently, lest you forget the things which your eyes have seen . . . make them known to your children and your children's children—how on the day that you stood before the LORD your God at Horeb, the LORD said to me, 'Gather the people to me, that I may let them hear my words, so that they may learn to fear me all the days that they live upon the earth, and that they may teach their children so'" (Deut. 4:2, 9–10).

Passing the faith from one generation to the next is a difficulty that I know from first-hand experience. My spiritual life, I recognize, is only a dim reflection of that of my father, an evangelical minister, although it is something I struggle over mightily. How do I pass along a vibrant faith to my own sons, whom I love more than life itself?

Evangelical youth organizations—Sunday schools, Bible camps, youth groups—fairly reverberate with testimonies about "rededication," and you don't have to hear too many of these rededication soliloquies to discern a pattern. The adolescents struggle to claim their parents' faith as their own. Some manage to grasp it, others fall by the way, and still others, I am convinced, go through a kind of ritualized rebellion during which they tell themselves—subconsciously, of course—that for their conversions to have any merit, they must be able, like their parents, to convert out of a life of sin.

"Sir I Labour under a hard heart & blind mind & what shall I say," John Loring wrote to his father. "I must beg that God of his Infinite mercy for his Sons Sake would Send down his Spirit on me to open mine eyes & soften my hard heart without which I shall perish . . . O Sir beg of God for me that he would doe these things for me & that the word dispensed from time to time might prove a savour of Life unto Life & not of death unto death but that it might be sharp & powerfull as a two edged sword." In yet another letter, John Loring wrote, "Begging your prayers that God would of his infinite mercy through Jesus Sake Send down his blessed Spirit to open my blind eyes & soften my hard heart so that I might be turned from darkness to Light and from the power of Sin & Satan unto God, so that I might sing of redeeming Love & Grace throughout the endless ages of eternity." Israel Loring, the father, felt similar anguish. On May 26, 1750, he wrote in his diary: "When Parents do with unceasing Fervour implore our good God, that he will please to do this good Unto their Children; to make them good, and Upright in heart; it is a Sign, that he will at Some time or other do it for them. May this passage Quicken me to call Upon God in the behalf of my Children as long as I live."

How do you pass the faith from one generation to the next? I can only speculate, but my guess would be that it entails faith and a whole lot of prayer, car washes and camping trips, Sunday school and catechism, and perhaps even some cajoling. "Train up a child in the way he should go," Proverbs enjoins us, "and when he is old he will not depart from it" (Prov. 22:6 RSV).

But let us not forget grace, that oft-neglected cornerstone of our faith. God, the great hound of heaven, somehow—through persistence, a kind of divine cunning, and even through our meager efforts—calls his children to himself. I know of no greater evidence of grace.

I do not know if John Loring's restless soul ever found the assurance he so desperately sought. After about 1750 the letters cease, there are some complaints about illness, and then the trail turns cold. I suspect, however, that a gracious God rescued him from his travail, either in this life or the next, not because of John Loring's anxiety or earnestness, but simply because of grace.

When I wrote the preface to my book on contemporary evangelicalism some years ago, I allowed myself to ruminate on the exemplary faith and piety of my parents, the ways I had disappointed them, and the ways in which my own piety had fallen shy of those standards. When it came time to dedicate book, I elected to dedicate it to my older son. "For Christian," I wrote, "who in time, I trust, will find his place in the patchwork quilt of American evangelicalism."

A large number of people have commented on that dedication, and I have come to see that the key word in that sentiment is *trust*. As a parent, as a frail and broken human being, I cannot secure my son's salvation, even though I would do everything in my power to do so. Instead, I must look to Jesus, who imparts grace in numberless ways, regardless of our merit. The best that I can do is to heed the words of Moses back there on the banks of the Jordan and pass along the stories of God's faithfulness from one generation to the next—the ways in which I have seen the hand of God: in protection from harm during a rock slide on a mountain in northern California or in a bicycle accident in Manhattan; in somehow getting me into a graduate school when there was very little in my record to suggest that I was qualified; in the gift of family; in allowing me to see the hand of God in the beauty of nature; in the sure and steady way that God has guided my steps through the years.

And within the community of faith, we regale one another with stories of God's faithfulness as well as our experience of the absence of God. We rehearse, both individually and collectively, the blessings and the epiphanies of faith through the years. Tell the stories of God's faithfulness—to ancient Israel and to the present day. "Take heed, and keep your soul diligently," as Moses said, "lest you forget the things which your eyes have seen, and lest they depart from your heart all the days of your life; make them known to your children and your children's children."

# GOSPEL AND GOSSIP

Therefore lift up your drooping hands and strengthen your
weak knees, and make straight paths for your feet, so that
what is lame may not be put out of joint but rather be healed.

HEBREWS 12:12–13 (RSV)

---

More than twenty years ago, when I learned that I had been
admitted to graduate school, I was eager to tell two of the
most important people in my life: my father and my mentor in seminary. My father was an evangelical minister who, as it
happens, attended but never graduated from seminary. My adviser
was a highly educated, kind, and pious man who had steered me
toward a master's thesis on the doctrine of biblical inerrancy.

I had expected both my father and my adviser to be delighted
by the improbable news that I had been admitted to an Ivy League
university. Instead, both greeted the news less than enthusiastically.
"You know," my adviser intoned ominously, "the people out there
are going to come after you on the issue of inerrancy." I had spent
the last several years working full-time at the seminary while pursuing my master's degree part-time, so I was well aware of how peo-

ple at this fundamentalist seminary had made the doctrine of biblical inerrancy the keystone of their entire theology. I also knew that they regarded their position as an embattled one, so I could expect to be persecuted for my defense of inerrancy.

My father, who was reared on a farm in Nebraska during the Great Depression, is not an expressive man, but I expected that he might betray at least a hint of satisfaction—even pride—that his son was going on to doctoral studies. But after hearing the news, he diverted his eyes and remained silent for a long time. I think I heard dishes clattering in the background. He cleared his throat and allowed only that he hoped my intellectual pursuits wouldn't compromise my piety.

Over the course of five years of graduate study, not one person inquired about my views on biblical inerrancy. The state of my piety, on the other hand, is not for me to judge; I leave that to others. But I am intrigued by these two reactions and by what they suggest about the state of evangelicalism and evangelical theology.

Let me lay my cards on the table. More than twenty years of personal reflection and a couple of decades studying evangelicalism in America have persuaded me that my father's comments are more germane than my adviser's—that evangelicalism stands to lose far more by surrendering its piety than it does by reexamining its theology. In fact, I have come to believe that if there is any hope for evangelicalism whatsoever, we must divest ourselves of some of our theological shibboleths—and the sooner the better.

For roughly the last century we evangelicals have imbibed Enlightenment standards of rationality for our theological discourse. That is, we have taken the simple "good news" of the New Testament— the revolutionary notion that the grace of God rescues us from the ravages of our own depravity—and we have dissected it and bent it and crammed it into rationalistic categories that we think will be acceptable to the intellectual community.

The irony here is that American evangelicals came rather late to Enlightenment-style argumentation. They were blindsided in the nineteenth century by Darwinism and Higher Criticism, a scholarly approach to the Bible that cast serious doubts on the reliability of the biblical texts. Taken together, Higher Criticism and Darwin's theory of evolution represented a frontal assault on the Scriptures, especially for those who insisted on literal interpretation. Evangelicals, particularly those who identify with the Reformed tradition, have been fighting back ever since. They sent their best students to secular universities to earn academic credentials and to joust with liberals and skeptics. And they have crafted rationalistic defenses of the faith, from the Princeton doctrine of biblical inerrancy to air-tight apologetics to excavations on Mount Ararat looking for Noah's Ark to exhaustive systematic theologies covering every theological contingency and answering every critic.

One reading of evangelical theology in the twentieth century is that evangelicals were obsessed with fighting the battles they lost a century earlier. They staved off challenges from every quarter—from modernism to Catholicism, from pentecostalism and evolution to the Death of God movement. When Karl Barth had the temerity to suggest that the Bible was not merely the Word of God, that the Bible *became* the Word of God as the Holy Spirit revealed it to the reader, evangelicals attacked Neo-Orthodoxy for being liberal, essentially because Barth's doctrine of Scripture was too soft for evangelical rationalists. Evangelical theologians have expended untold energies responding to the assaults of Enlightenment skeptics. They have constructed an intellectual fortress that is logically impenetrable. They have cut and sliced and proof-texted. They have stripped all mystery from the Bible, this wonderfully complicated and maddeningly contradictory book, and they have given us a theology that is airtight and unambiguous and intellectually defensible—and cold and sterile and deadly dull, about as interesting and compelling and nutritious as a dollop of Cool Whip.

In some respects it is difficult to criticize this impulse. All theology, after all, is temporal; that is, while truth may be immutable, theology—literally, the study of God—represents a particular, time-bound understanding of that truth. The content of Paul's letters to the early Christians, for example, was determined in part by the circumstances surrounding the first-century church. St. Augustine's magisterial *City of God* was written in the context of the decline of the Roman Empire, and Martin Luther's theology would have taken far different form were it not for the emergence of nation-states in Europe.

Although they often confused theology with truth, evangelical theologians of the twentieth century nevertheless succeeded admirably in responding to attacks from Enlightenment rationalism. Just as the Chuck Norris and Sylvester Stallone movies replay the war in Vietnam so that the United States can claim at least a celluloid victory, so too evangelicals have replayed the intellectual battles they lost a century ago. And, lest anyone think otherwise, they won this time. They won decisively. The logic was better, the arguments superior, the footnotes longer and more persuasive.

The only problem, however, is that no one was mounting a counterargument any longer. For better or worse—for better, in my judgment—the canons of the Enlightenment began to fall out of favor in the waning decades of the twentieth century. Postmodernism insists that there are no fixed standards of truth, and feminism has taught us the importance of taking our own stories as a point of departure in the quest for meaning.

With its insistence on hewing to rationalistic categories, however, evangelical theology is sadly out of step with the spirit of the age. When people ask how they can imbue their lives with meaning, evangelicals have responded with lectures about biblical authority or disquisitions about the tripartite division of the soul. When people at the turn of the twenty-first century look for evidence of the presence of God, evangelicals unfurl their eschatological charts and wax eloquent about the tribulation and the seventy weeks of Daniel.

It's time to reconsider the theological enterprise, time to imagine an evangelical theology in a new key. That would entail a

44

frank recognition that truth and theology are two different enti-
ties—one is timeless and immutable, and the other is temporal
and fallible. I have no illusions about writing the theology for the
ages; what intrigues me is the possibility of writing a theology for
this age.

What might that theology look like? There is, I am told, an ety-
mological relationship between the words *gospel* and *gossip*. If we allow
ourselves to take that observation seriously, the first four books of
the New Testament begin to look different from the way we've viewed
them in the past. If we could for just a moment suppress our impulse
to scream "Blasphemy!" at the very thought, we might say that the
Gospels contain gossip—people telling stories to one another, the
stories of a few simple fishermen and their encounter with Jesus. If
we allow ourselves the additional impiety of noting that a story is a
tricky matter, that it lies somewhere near the intersection of truth
and memory, we free ourselves from the tedious task of what theologians call "harmonizing the Gospels," making sure that everyone
tells the story the same way. The story of the nativity, then, or the
feeding of the five thousand becomes less a matter of counting heads
than appreciating the miracle that God became man or compre-
hending the awesome spectacle of a preacher who was willing to sus-
pend his sermon long enough to attend, miraculously, to the physical needs of his auditors.

Viewing the Gospels as gossip, a collection of stories, might be
construed as an invitation to tell our own stories and even to weave
our own narratives into the narrative of the New Testament. I confess, for example, that as a Sunday school alumnus the doctrine of
grace was a rather abstract notion until I encountered firm and
irrefutable evidence of my own sinfulness; I now sing "Amazing
Grace, How Sweet the Sound!" with a gusto I could never have imag-
ined as a twelve-year-old. What theologians call the passion of
Christ, the events leading to his crucifixion, remained academic for
me before I knew first-hand about abandonment and desolation.

This evangelical theology in a new key, one that sets aside ratio-nalistic argumentation in favor of narrative, opens new possibilities. We might take the notion that Jesus was fully human, for example, as an invitation to be fully human ourselves. That entails accepting ourselves, with all of our blemishes, just as Jesus has accepted us. Being human also means that we have our own narratives, and each of us in the community of faith can learn from others. In the words of Terry Tempest Williams, "We are healed by our stories."

If I told you, for example, that my struggle to claim the faith over the last several decades has involved a titanic struggle with my own father, that account might resonate with some of you. I could speak in rather abstract terms about the theological virtues of duty and honor and obedience, and I might even invoke the parable of the prodigal son, but if I related an incident or two from my childhood, you might be freed to offer your own stories.

I could, to take another example, regale you with yet another tedious discussion about God's will or the theological niceties of the doctrine of calling and vocation. Alternatively, I could tell you about the three-foot-tall wooden pulpit in the basement of my parents' home in Des Moines, Iowa. That miniature pulpit was built more than forty years ago by a carpenter in my father's congregation in East Chain, Minnesota. It was modeled after the church's pulpit, and it was my Christmas present a couple of months following my fifth birthday.

Anyone who is a parent knows that Christmas is a season of great anxiety, wondering how your children will react to their gifts. I assure you that my pulpit was a source of great delight for me—but even more for my parents, because they saw it as a symbol of my calling. Countless family pictures show a bedimpled and bespeckled five-year-old pounding his pulpit and preaching for all he's worth. My calling, my father had decided, was to be a preacher, to follow in his foot-steps and eventually to assume his mantle, to carry on the noble tra-dition of preaching the gospel.

As I look back on it now I see that my teenage years were a kind of training camp. Quite willingly, I became president of the youth group, I trotted off to Bible camp every summer, and I generally stayed out of trouble during those perilous high school years until I arrived safely at an evangelical college, my faith untainted and my theology intact.

I even have a vague recollection that I won a preaching competition somewhere during those years, but any preaching I did was purely imitative and, therefore, disastrous, merely an empty recitation of the party line. I knew what I was supposed to say, and I knew what people wanted to hear, so I obliged them shamelessly.

To this day I mark the beginning of my transition from adolescence to adulthood to a conversation—a confrontation, really—with my father in his study. It was a beautiful spring afternoon just weeks before my college graduation. Although I had recently announced my intention to marry a "good Christian girl," I had also decided against entering seminary that fall, and my father summoned me to his office to set me back on course for my career in the ministry.

"Your mother and I want you to start seminary this fall," he said tonelessly. "We've even decided to help you with the cost of tuition."

I couldn't bear to look at him just then, but I could hear the pain and disappointment in his voice as he blustered through a speech about calling and God's will that I'm sure he had rehearsed a hundred times that morning. There is nothing I wanted more than to acquiesce, but I also knew my own anguish. I had serious reservations about my fitness for the ministry, and I knew that if I continued to follow the course my father had charted for me the succession of expectations would never end. I held my ground, not without difficulty, and when I left the study that afternoon more than twenty-five years ago, my father and I went our separate ways.

Oh, we maintained a strained cordiality, we saw one another at Christmas and other occasions, but the letters we had exchanged while I had been away at college stopped abruptly; we no longer had very much to say to one another. Curiously—or perhaps not so curiously—I pursued a parallel career path, although I didn't recognize it at the time. I did in fact attend seminary, but I earned an M.A. degree rather than a divinity degree; I chose the podium rather than the pulpit.

My father stayed his course, pursuing the peripatetic life of a preacher. My parents moved from Iowa to Minnesota to Illinois to California and finally back to Iowa to retire. The three-foot-tall pulpit has followed them everywhere. Crafted by the sturdy hands of a carpenter, it has gathered dust in the basements of nearly a dozen houses.

I can only speculate about what that pulpit symbolized for my parents over the years. It evoked an overwhelming nostalgia, I expect, but it also represented dashed hopes and expectations, not to mention unanswered prayers. The pulpit for me was a reproach; I winced whenever I saw it. It also represented everything I found coercive and stultifying about evangelicalism.

Because I am not ordained, because I have never taken a homiletics course, because I am not a preacher, I don't receive many invitations to preach. I rarely decline an offer, however; something compels me to accept.

More often than not, I use that opportunity to talk about grace, for it is my observation that evangelicals speak all too rarely about grace. I preach about grace because I have come to believe the gospel assurances that grace overwhelms the law, and that sounds like good news to me indeed.

I preach about grace because I have seen the workings of grace in numberless ways—in the unspeakable gift of two sons, in a career that has flourished beyond my wildest expectations, in the gift of love and companionship on the far side of a wrenching divorce.

I preach about grace because in all the years of listening to my father preach I never heard a sermon so eloquent as when he flew across the country to sit quietly by my bedside several years ago as I lay suspended between life and death. That silent gesture was suffused with reconciliation and forgiveness and redemption and grace, and I learned more about theology in those days and weeks than I ever did in three years of seminary.

I preach about grace because, in the end, nothing much matters other than grace.

My preaching, I fear, is rather different from my father's. It is nuanced and textured, sometimes tortured, and it lacks the self-confidence I hear in most evangelical sermons. That might have been different, I suspect, had I followed the trajectory prescribed for me.

My father, I believe, was right all those years ago: We have far more to fear from losing our piety than our theology. I would be hard-pressed to articulate my own theology, especially to do so in the conventional categories of evangelical rationalism. For me, any theology worthy of the name has been forged out of the crucible of experience, tempered by pain and disappointment and failure, because only then can we begin to comprehend the miracle of grace.

I call myself an evangelical because I dare to believe that the gospel of the New Testament is good news indeed, that Jesus takes our sad, broken lives and somehow makes us whole. I dare to believe that the narrative of the Gospels lends structure and meaning to our own fractured narratives. I even dare to believe that for all the hope and disappointment that it symbolizes, the three-foot-tall pulpit gathering dust in my parents' basement may have a purpose after all, there may be a lesson I don't yet comprehend about redemption and reconciliation, even grace.

"We are healed by our stories."

49

# FINISHING THE COURSE

And Moses went up from the plains of Moab to Mount Nebo, to the top of Pisgah, which is opposite Jericho. And the LORD showed him all the land, Gilead as far as Dan, all Naphtali, the land of Ephraim and Manasseh, all the land of Judah as far as the Western Sea, the Negeb, and the Plain, that is, the valley of Jericho the city of palm trees, as far as Zoar. And the LORD said to him, "This is the land of which I swore to Abraham, to Isaac, and to Jacob, 'I will give it to your descendants.' I have let you see it with your eyes, but you shall not go over there." So Moses the servant of the LORD died there in the land of Moab, according to the word of the LORD, and he buried him in the valley in the land of Moab opposite Beth-peor; but no man knows the place of his burial to this day. Moses was a hundred and twenty years old when he died; his eye was not dim, nor his natural force abated. And the people of Israel wept for Moses in the plains of Moab thirty days; then the days of weeping and mourning for Moses were ended.

And Joshua the son of Nun was full of the spirit of wisdom, for Moses had laid his hands upon him; so the people of Israel obeyed him, and did as the LORD had commanded Moses. And there has not arisen a prophet since in Israel like Moses, whom

the LORD knew face to face, none like him for all the signs and
the wonders which the LORD sent him to do in the land of
Egypt, to Pharoah and to all his servants and to all his land,
and for all the mighty power and all the great and terrible
deeds which Moses wrought in the sight of all Israel.

DEUTERONOMY 34:1–12 (RSV)

A fter a long and (to say the least) eventful life, Moses reached
the end of his days. The man who had been born into servi-
tude and abandoned in the bullrushes, who had been reared
in Pharoah's household and yet chose to identify with his own people, the man who, with knees shaking, saw God in the burning bush
and obeyed the summons to lead his people out of bondage to the
promised land—this man had collected ancient Israel's equivalent
of a gold watch and was deep into retirement. Such an extraordinary life: the epic confrontations with Pharoah, communicating the
message to "let my people go," ten horrible plagues, the wanderings
in the wilderness—a cloud by day and a pillar of fire by night—the
parting of the Red Sea, the hike up Mount Sinai, then that ugly incident with the golden calf, and all the while having to hear more
whining and complaining than a doctor's office waiting room.
"There's not enough to eat!" "Where's our water?" It was enough to
make you hang up your staff and call it a day.

Which, in a way, is what Moses did, though not voluntarily.
Deuteronomy tells us that Moses, even at the age of 120 years, possessed all of his faculties. His mind was sharp and his eyes clear
enough finally, after all those years, to glimpse the promised land—
from his prospect atop Mount Nebo across the Jordan River.

Therein lies the real story. After leading the Israelites through
the wilderness, after putting up with the endless caterwauling,

Moses was not allowed to step foot in the promised land. He had to view it from afar.

Why? The Bible tells us that Jahweh, the God of ancient Israel, denied Moses' visa because Moses had disobeyed. He had struck the rock rather than speaking to it, and for that God had banished Moses from the promised land, this long-awaited territory flowing with milk and honey.

I think I decided some time ago that I didn't much care for the tough-guy God of the Hebrew Bible. He seems petulant and disagreeable much of the time, a guy with a hair-trigger temper. I much prefer the God of the New Testament, mediated—and modulated—through Jesus. We live now under the aegis of grace rather than the law, and the rules have changed, but I wonder if we might find a lesson or two in the account of Moses' demise here in Deuteronomy.

What strikes me first is what I shall call the horseshoe phenomenon, deriving from that old saw that *close* counts only in horseshoes and hand grenades. Moses came close—ever so close—to his goal, but he could not finish the course. He had to view the promised land from afar, and I wonder how many of us (and I include myself in this category) fall just short of the mark in our Christian lives. How many of us know the notes but can't play the music? We are reluctant to take that leap of faith or to embrace it fully and with abandon. We're too cautious, or we fear the derision of our peers, or we live too much inside of our heads. I know the arguments. "The time isn't right." "I already believe; what more do you want?" And so, like Moses, we miss out on the great adventure of faith. We can *see* the promised land of faith, that marvelous gift of being able to confess Jesus as Lord, but we cannot touch it or feel it. We can know it only from afar and thereby miss out on spiritual intimacy.

The New Testament also contains a kind of parallel valedictory, when Paul recounts the course he had taken. He seems a trifle defensive at times, but we know to expect that from Paul. He asserts that he had acted uprightly and had spoken the gospel boldly. Paul writes elsewhere about running the race and finishing the course, metaphors of athleticism that have been picked up at various times throughout church history, from the monks to the missionaries, from the Crusades to the Promise Keepers. Life is a journey, a pilgrimage, fraught at times with perils; witness *Pilgrim's Progress*, by John Bunyan. But the message is the same: Jesus helps us negotiate the many perils along our way and guides us safely home. Jesus helps us to finish the course.

I'm not enough of a theologian to know how this applies to Moses, standing forlornly there on Mount Nebo gazing into the middle distance across the Jordan, his eyes somewhat misty, I imagine, as he contemplates what might have been. But I know that, through the agency of Jesus, we live now in the age of grace rather than the law, and I have to believe that Jesus, God become man, would have found a way to bring Moses safely across Jordan to the promised land.

I was traveling several weeks ago when the message arrived that a childhood friend of mine had checked into a motel room and suffocated himself. Marc was born to loving and godly parents, who reared him in the faith. They took him and his siblings to Sunday school and sent them to Bible camp. They *lived* their faith rather than merely preaching it, and their faith had sustained them through more illness and tragedy than any family should have to bear—a stillborn child, another who died in infancy, a son who passed away from a sudden illness at the age of six.

Marc's family and my family had been the best of friends when we lived in Michigan many years ago. Marc was several years older than I, and I admired him enormously. He was bright and handsome and muscular and athletic, and I wanted to be like him. I even recall, at age eleven or so, trying to discipline myself to lower my voice and stick out my chest so I could be like Marc. He had a nice car and a motorcycle and always, it seemed, a pretty girl on his arm. He took me skiing one day, and while I fumbled down the slopes in my hopelessly out-of-fashion corduroy coat, Marc was careening expertly in his ski pants and matching jacket. Marc was like a god to me; I thought the world of him.

Marc wanted to be a surgeon, a heart surgeon, but for reasons I never learned that didn't work out. He went through a hippie phase out in California and then, almost as quickly, a stint with the Jesus People. He married a lovely woman—a "good Christian girl," as we used to say—and they had a son, but somewhere along the path he lost his way. This enormously talented man went through a succession of jobs, a divorce, law school but no bar exam, still more jobs. He was wandering in the wilderness. He knew the notes, but he couldn't play the music.

I lost track of Marc some years ago, and I wish now that I had been more persistent in my attempts to find him. But he had distanced himself from those who loved him, including his parents and his two sisters. Wandering alone in the wilderness, looking for some elusive promised land, until his parents received a phone call asking them to come identify the body lying in the morgue of a strange and distant city.

One of the many reasons that I am not an ordained minister is that I don't know how to comfort grieving parents and siblings in a tragedy like this, but I had to try. We agreed on what a shame it was, what wasted talent and potential. We tried to find words for the unspeakable sadness that had enveloped all who loved him. We even talked about the selfishness of such an action, how it left everyone else to deal with the consequences, but I knew that the underlying—and overwhelming—anxiety centered around Marc and the state of his soul. He knew the path, but he had lost his way, wandering there in the wilderness.

I have no way of knowing what thoughts raced through his mind as his world finally collapsed around him. Like Moses, perhaps, and like all of us someday, he may have reviewed his life and his own

55

wanderings, tallied his gains and losses. "He has a lot to account for," his mother told me amid her tears. Don't we all—Moses and Paul and all of us? But we are fortunate to have in Jesus not only an advocate but a fellow traveler, and the ability to confess him as Lord on *this* side of the Jordan is the greatest of all earthly gifts.

Jesus takes our wanderings and our waywardness and somehow, through the miracle of grace, makes them his own. The message of the gospel is that, despite our fears and our reluctance and our inability to confess, Jesus gives direction to our steps and helps us to finish the course. In the ultimate triumph of grace over law, he guides us safely home.

Jesus calls his children safely home.

# KEEPING FAITH

And Jesus said to him, "If you can! All things are possible to
him who believes." Immediately the father of the child cried
out and said, "I believe; help my unbelief!"

MARK 9:23-24 (RSV)

---

Dear Mr. Balmer:

I think it was the campfire scene that convinced me
to write. At Camp Woodworth we threw pinecones. The
night air smelled like the sea and smoke and the sweat
of too many tired children at the end of a long day. Like
Carl and Amy, like you, we too shuffled our feet in the
sand and picked nervously at our tennis shoes as we
watched and waited to see who would testify next. That
was a long time ago. But today I was there again,
transported through time by your words.

Thank you for writing that book. I laughed out loud, I gritted my teeth, I mourned, I guffawed, I wept. And I felt a kindred spirit in you. I felt not alone.

Yours sincerely, Kris

Dear Mr. Balmer,

I have just finished your book, *Mine Eyes Have Seen the Glory*. It is very reassuring to realize that I'm not alone in my journey with God, and that others have had a similar walk through life.

Sincerely, Janet

Dear Dr. Balmer:

I heard an interview with you on National Public Radio about a month ago. . . . I almost started to cry when I heard you talk about the difficulties of growing up evangelical. I have been struggling with this for years now and feel like very few people can understand these difficulties. After all these years of being a Christian, I still have a little faith and a lot of questions. I am still scared to death to find out that evangelical Christianity is not true. The message of the gospel still makes a lot of sense to me, but I cannot separate what is mine from what is part of what you call the evangelical subculture. I do not want to disappoint all my friends, and the prospect of having to leave my church is overwhelming at times.

I am not sure why I am writing this letter other than, after hearing your interview, I think you are one of the people who can understand what I am going through. If you have any words of wisdom or advice that you feel like passing on, I would be glad to listen.

Sincerely, Jeffrey

I have several files of letters. Most of them begin like the ones I have just quoted, with some expression of identification or solidarity, even appreciation. "How is it that you know me?" one letter begins. Many correspondents suggest that, in the course of describing my own pilgrimage as an evangelical, I was also telling their stories. Some of them offer details about their faith journeys—page after single-spaced page—and I am left to wonder why anyone would disclose such intimate secrets to a stranger.

But there is yet another element in many of these letters, and it concerns the matter of faith, the subject of the passage from the Gospel of Mark. Some writers detect in me a lack of faith and urge me to embrace the fundamentalism of my childhood; they assure me that they are praying for me—something for which I am always grateful. A good many more correspondents, however, talk wistfully about a faith that they have lost, or at least misplaced. They profess admiration for someone who they perceive has managed to hold onto the faith, and they ask how I have succeeded in doing so.

That makes me, I confess, a trifle uneasy. Evangelicalism already has far too many heroes—big, flashy athletes and musicians and missionaries and preachers who, to hear them tell it, have never suffered a moment's doubt or fear or uncertainty since their own thunderous conversions many years earlier. I wish these superheroes well, and I congratulate them on their confidence. But they don't inhabit the same planet I do.

I am no hero. Jeffrey needs to understand that. I refuse the nomination—in the words of William Tecumseh Sherman, if nominated I will not run; if elected I will not serve—and so I'm never sure how to answer these letters. I want to do so carefully, for I feel as though I am dealing with something important, even precious. So once I sit down and pound out "Dear Jeffrey: Thank you for your kind letter and for taking the time to write" I generally stare for a while at the computer screen, wondering what to say next.

What I say next is that I understand Jeffrey's quandary. And I do. One of the most difficult challenges for any religion is passing the faith from one generation to the next. This is especially true within a tradition that places a great deal of emphasis on religious fervor and a conversion experience. For me, the single most important epiphany in writing *Mine Eyes Have Seen the Glory* occurred when I visited Word of Life Camp in Schroon Lake, New York. As I talked to the teenage campers and listened to the sermons and Bible studies, my own life finally began to make sense to me. For the first time I understood that my parents, having been converted in a dramatic fashion out of what they regarded as a sinful past, wanted the same for me. But because I had been socialized in the church since infancy—Sunday school, youth group, Bible camp, Christian college—I had no sinful past to speak of out of which to convert. "Giving my life to Jesus" seemed like an empty exercise because I was merely ratifying the beliefs and the lifestyle that my parents had drilled into me. My conversion didn't live up to my own expectations, and so I returned to Bible camp summer after summer and rededicated my life to Jesus time after time after time. Staring into the campfire through moistened eyes, I tried desperately to conjure the right emotions so that I could convince my parents and my peers and, most important, myself that I was firmly and finally "saved."

Jeffrey, my correspondent, understands this, I think. I suspect that he, like so many other evangelical kids I know, went through a phase late in adolescence that I have come to call "ritualized rebellion." Having tried again and again to appropriate an acceptable conversion experience, we undertake some sort of reaction—usually it's fairly half-hearted—during which we convince ourselves (subconsciously, at least) that we have a sordid past out of which to convert. This will make our Sunday-evening testimonies more compelling in later years.

Many evangelical adolescents eventually do find their way back to the fold, and many are probably better for the experience; they feel more settled or centered perhaps, having sown a few wild oats. Others never return to the warm bosom of evangelicalism. They become overwhelmed by what evangelicals used to call "worldliness" or they attend an evangelical college and drift off to graduate school, which brings me to my second response to Jeffrey's letter.

Education. I detect in many of the letters I have received in recent years an undercurrent of surprise that someone with academic credentials and Ivy League affiliations actually believes in Jesus. That sentiment, I suppose, is understandable. Indeed, after more years of study than I care to count, I can recite for you the sociological, anthropological, and psychoanalytical explanations for religious behavior. I can explain the quest for a deity as the search for a father figure or as a response to social upheaval. Most college sophomores, I expect, could do the same.

The evangelical response to these intellectual challenges has been, in my judgment, utterly misguided. To these arguments about religious belief, informed by Enlightenment rationalism, evangelicals mounted counterarguments, also informed by Enlightenment rationalism. Evangelicals sent their best and most trustworthy students off to Cambridge and Harvard and Tübingen, and those who managed to return to the subculture with their doctorates in hand and largely unaffected by the experience were hailed as role models for having emerged from the lions' den unscathed. These "doctors" were then paraded like show dogs in front of impressionable young evangelicals and told to teach courses in apologetics.

Somehow, I don't think Jeffrey wants me to rehearse the ontological, the teleological, and the cosmological arguments for the existence of God. Enlightenment rationalism has fallen out of favor these days, even in the universities, as people grope for meaning rather than mere method. So instead of dusting off the teleological argument, I think I'll remind Jeffrey about Karl Barth, arguably the most important theologian of the twentieth century. Toward the end of his life, after he had written volume after volume on the transcendence of God and the centrality of Jesus, Barth was asked to sum up his work. The good doctor paused for a minute and no doubt looked out the window and played with the stubble on his chin before responding with the words of a Sunday school ditty: "Jesus loves me, this I know, for the Bible tells me so."

Jeffrey, I think, will appreciate that story, and I'll remind him again of the passage in the Gospel of Mark, the utterance of the father of a young boy, at once forlorn and hopeful: "I believe; help my unbelief!"

There is another element to this passage that I find intriguing, the suggestion that faith is somehow collaborative. We Protestants learned from Augustine and Calvin a long time ago that human agency is flawed by the sin we inherited from Adam, and so the distraught father in the Gospel, having declared his faith, must, in the next breath, enlist help in sustaining his faith. Jesus honors such appeals; indeed, he makes them possible, but there is a wider possibility here, the possibility that we in the community of faith help one another with our unbelief. In moments of intellectual or physical or emotional crisis, we turn to one another for help in the midst of our unbelief. We Protestants have enlarged the notion of sainthood to include all fellow believers, so perhaps this is what we mean when we talk about "the communion of the saints." We don't have to conjure images of beatific countenances that passed from this earth centuries ago; we can look to one another in the community of faith for help in our unbelief.

This "collaborative faith," however, requires something that is in short supply among evangelicals: honesty. Evangelicals are big on truth, especially propositional truth: biblical inerrancy, the authenticity of miracles, the teleological argument for the existence of God. But honesty is a very different matter from truth. It requires openness and disclosure and vulnerability. The words *gospel* and *gossip* derive from the same root, so perhaps we should read the New Testament as an invitation to offer our own narratives to the community of faith. This means telling stories about ourselves and listening to the stories of others without censure or condemnation, without responding with pieties or proof-texts. Truth (of a sort) is rampant in evangelicalism; honesty is in short supply. Lord, have mercy.

Perhaps that is why Janet and Kris and Jeffrey have written to me, why they are willing to spill their secrets to someone they have never met. They detect in me a fellow pilgrim, someone who has had more than his share of stumbles along the way, and who might be willing to disclose a part of himself, to tell his story.

In the end, that's about all I have to offer Jeffrey. I'll assure him that he is not alone and that I periodically have my own crises of faith, times when doubt seems far more reasonable than belief. Yes, Jeffrey, if I may quote you, "I still have a little faith and a lot of questions." But somehow, by grace and through the ministrations of fellow pilgrims—the communion of the saints—I mean to persevere. And perhaps, in a year or a month or sometime next week when I am enduring my own dark night of the soul, I'll call on Jeffrey for help. The communion of the saints.

Yes, Jeffrey, I believe. Help my unbelief!

# DISCERNING THE CALL

Now the boy Samuel was ministering to the LORD under Eli. And the word of the LORD was rare in those days; there was no frequent vision.

At that time Eli, whose eyesight had begun to grow dim, so that he could not see, was lying down in his own place; the lamp of God had not yet gone out, and Samuel was lying down within the temple of the LORD, where the ark of God was. Then the LORD called, "Samuel! Samuel!" and he said, "Here I am!" and ran to Eli, and said, "Here I am, for you called me." But he said, "I did not call, my son; lie down again." So he went and lay down. And the LORD called again, "Samuel!" And Samuel arose and went to Eli, and said, "Here I am, for you called me." But he said, "I did not call, my son; lie down again." Now Samuel did not yet know the LORD, and the word of the LORD had not yet been revealed to him. And the LORD called Samuel again the third time. And he arose and went to Eli, and said, "Here I am, for you called me." Then Eli perceived that the LORD was calling the boy. Therefore Eli said to Samuel, "Go, lie down; and if he calls you, you shall say, 'Speak, LORD, for thy servant hears.'" So Samuel went and lay down in his place.

And the LORD came and stood forth, calling as at other times, "Samuel! Samuel!" And Samuel said, "Speak, for thy servant hears."

1 SAMUEL 3:1–10 (RSV)

For me, one of the perils of being a preacher's kid was dealing with missionaries on furlough. Not only did it mean giving up my bedroom and sleeping on the living-room floor for a night or two or even a week, it meant listening to stories about the dangers of life in the bush, admonitions about "fields white unto harvest," and watching an overexposed slide show. The visit of missionaries invariably concluded with an altar call, a summons to missionary service, as the congregation sang verse after endless verse:

> I'll go where You want me to go, dear Lord,
> Over mountain, or plain, or sea.
> I'll say what You want me to say, dear Lord.
> I'll be what You want me to be.

Many tears flowed during that concluding altar call—tears of the few who ventured down the aisle, their parents (either from pride or fear, I could never tell which), and those of us who felt guilty for not stepping forward to obey the call of God to the mission field.

The truth was, I didn't much care for snakes, especially the nasty, venomous kind that lurked in the African bush, so I couldn't in all honesty sing "I'll go where You want me to go, dear Lord," because I was fairly sure he'd want me to go somewhere in the vicinity of those vipers.

Samuel faced a similar fate, I suppose, a kind of snakepit. It was not the best of times for the Israelites; they were sorely in need of a prophet, and the clergy had fallen into corruption. "Word from the LORD was rare in those days," the Bible tells us, "visions were infrequent" (1 Sam. 3:1 NASB). Small wonder that young Samuel repeatedly mistook the call of God for the voice of Eli, his mentor. It took God three times to get through, but Samuel finally answered, even though at that time, the Scriptures say, "Samuel did not yet know the LORD, nor had the word of the LORD yet been revealed to him" (1 Sam. 3:7 NASB). But Samuel nevertheless heard the call. The call was definite, and his answer unambiguous: "Speak, for Your servant is listening" (1 Sam. 3:10 NASB).

I find Samuel's story enviable. Noises in the night can be rather disquieting, of course, but once we learn the provenance we can rest easier. Samuel heard the voice—and, after some initial confusion, he knew it was God's. The Almighty appeared to Moses in a burning bush and to Saul on the road to Damascus. Very little ambiguity there. Augustine of Hippo had no trouble making out the call of God; Martin Luther was struck down in a thunderstorm in the German countryside; and a bolt of lightning struck Gilbert Tennent, one of the revivalists of the Great Awakening, while he was preparing a sermon in his study.

Most of us, however, live in a more ambiguous world, and some of us, I dare say, have been struggling with the notion of calling—or vocation—for much of our lives. We wrestle with such issues as duty and responsibility, hubris and humility, personal identity and parental expectations.

When I look back now, I can see that my life had been scripted. As the eldest son of an evangelical minister, it fell to me to carry on the family business—to attend an evangelical college, move on to seminary, then ordination and a succession of ever larger congregations. Somewhere along the line, however, I fell out of step, searching for something else—not better, necessarily, but different. While I recognize that one of the job descriptions for adolescents is to confound and to disappoint their parents, I have come only lately to recognize how thoroughly I dashed my father's hopes.

As I was sorting through a box of old papers after a recent move, I came across several letters from my father. "We will be praying that the Lord will lead you into the vocation that He has reserved especially for you," my father wrote in a high school graduation card, and at the bottom of the card a biblical reference, Proverbs 3:5–6. After all those years of Sunday school I knew it from memory: "Trust in the Lord with all your heart, and lean not on your own understanding. In all your ways acknowledge Him and He shall direct your paths" (NKJV). My father choked back the tears as I headed out the driveway and off to college. "Doesn't seem right that your room downstairs is empty," he wrote later, but I knew that he took comfort from the knowledge that I would be well-positioned to hear the call of God and to respond affirmatively.

But, as often happens during those formative years, I moved in a different direction, not so much out of rebellion as out of curiosity. Reared in a household that was conservative and nominally Republican, I became a liberal Democrat. Although there had been a time when I determined to pass up college altogether, I became enamored of the life of the mind. The world was opening up to me, and I began to consider possibilities for my life other than becoming a minister. I called into question the whole notion of calling; it seemed vaguely mystical and intellectually soft. And, for the first time in my life, I began finding things to do on Sunday mornings other than church.

Although I could never have given voice to it at the time, I suspect that what I found off-putting about the missionary altar calls and the pressure I felt from my father was their contrived nature. They struck me as coercive and manipulative, and the course they prescribed seemed formulaic. Inevitably, my father and I drifted apart, and as college graduation approached he was seized, I think, with a kind of panic as his hopes and expectations began to crumble. During spring break of that final semester, my father summoned me to his office—for the first and the last time—and pressured me to attend seminary in the fall. He tried to look resolute, but his eyes were dark and fearful as he laid out his proposal, which included his library, moral and prayer support, and all the financial assistance he could manage.

To this day, I look back on that moment as a turning point, the beginning of my transition from adolescence to adulthood. I had to say no, of course; to answer otherwise would have meant subjecting myself to a lifetime of parental expectations. I had been reading Carl Rogers in those days, and *I'm O.K., You're O.K.* Something called "self-actualization" was all the rage. But the trauma of that encounter in my father's study left me trembling for days afterward. I had charted my own uncertain course, but I had also left him reeling and wounded.

The call I heard was rather different. It led to graduate school and teaching, but it doesn't take a psychiatrist to recognize the similarity between a lectern and a pulpit. Still, despite professional successes and a deepening commitment to the faith, my father thought I had missed my calling, that I had settled for second best. We sustained a kind of strained cordiality over the years, but the letters that had arrived regularly in my college mailbox containing news about my younger brothers, a Bible verse, and confidences about the challenges of the pastorate stopped altogether—not, I think, out of anger or because he sought to punish me, but simply because he no longer knew what to say.

My father and I staggered toward a kind of rapprochement about the time he reached retirement, two stubborn, wizened warriors finally grown tired of the duel. My father took delight in his grandsons and even, I think, began to take pride in his son, while I began to ponder the unthinkable: to consider what form a call to ministry might take.

Which brings me back to the story of Samuel. There are few stories more familiar to those of us reared in Sunday school than

Samuel and Eli and the call of God, and even now, at a remove of several decades, I can picture the cutout figure of Samuel, lantern in hand, staggering sleepily back and forth across the flannelgraph to Eli's room, trying to figure out who was calling him and why.

The moral of the story was simple. When God calls us we must obey and be prepared to follow that call, even to the jungles of Africa, and it was pretty much understood that God called only to the ministry or to missionary service.

The last time I heard the story of Samuel and Eli it was the devotional reading for a Sunday morning late in February. My family and I were in a hotel room, and I was scheduled to address the adult forum for a church I had attended while in graduate school. The message light was blinking upon our return to the hotel, and when I reached my brother the news was brief and altogether expected. "This is it," he said. "You better get here right away."

My father had been retired only four months when we moved my parents into the new house one of my brothers had built for their retirement. The following week we got the news that he was ill, and as the cancer spread stealthily through his body, we recognized that he would never use the workbench full of power tools we had given him to celebrate his retirement.

I cannot fully reconstruct my thoughts as I boarded the plane for that final journey to his bedside, but I remembered our encounter in his study those many years ago and how that encounter had left both of us confused and wounded. I envied the way he had kept the faith over the years, how he never doubted his calling as a minister of the gospel through all the sermon preparations and committee meetings and building programs and countless trips to the hospital. The airport in Cincinnati was deserted when I changed planes that Sunday night; Dan Fogelberg was singing "The Leader of the Band" over the sound system, and I caught the last plane to Des Moines. I rehearsed my own anxieties over the notion of calling and my gnawing sense of unworthiness. And I recalled the marvelous way in which grace had overwhelmed the law in my father's final months—how we had reached the point of reconciliation and how much I would miss him. I resolved to tell him that, if I were given the chance, and I resolved to assure him that, no matter how circuitous or unconventional, yes, I too had heard the call, and I was prepared to listen now—freely and joyfully, without constraint.

When I arrived just after ten o'clock, the last of his five sons, he was floating in and out of consciousness but, to quote from the story about Samuel, "the lamp of God had not yet gone out" (1 Sam. 3:3 RSV). He seemed to respond as I related my news, and my brothers commented that he seemed remarkably content and peaceful for the remaining half dozen hours of his life.

For me, the call of God has become only slightly clearer since we laid my father to rest beneath the wintry Iowa sky, and it has occurred to me that just as Samuel heard God's call only after he had ascertained that it was God calling, not Eli, I was also able to discern a call only after I recognized that the voice was God's and not that of my father. Still, some days I am overwhelmed by a sense of inadequacy; I wonder how the Almighty could possibly make any use out of a flawed vessel like me. But just as the Scriptures tell us that "Samuel did not yet know the LORD, and the word of the LORD had not yet been revealed to him" (1 Sam. 3:7 RSV), God also demands no prerequisites, only a willingness to hear: "Speak, for Your servant is listening."

71

# SINS OF THE FATHERS

"And these words which I command you this day shall be upon your heart; and you shall teach them diligently to your children, and shall talk of them when you sit in your house, and when you walk by the way, and when you lie down, and when you rise. And you shall bind them as a sign upon your hand, and they shall be as frontlets between your eyes. And you shall write them on the doorposts of your house and on your gates.

"When your son asks you in time to come, 'What is the meaning of the testimonies and the statutes and the ordinances which the LORD our God has commanded you?' then you shall say to your son, 'We were Pharoah's slaves in Egypt; and the LORD brought us out of Egypt with a mighty hand; and the LORD showed signs and wonders, great and grievous, against Egypt and against Pharoah and all his household, before our eyes; and he brought us out from there, that he might bring us in and give us the land which he swore to give to our fathers.'"

DEUTERONOMY 6:6–9, 20–23 (RSV)

73

T his is a story about fathers and sons.

My grandfather was the black sheep of his family back in Switzerland, as I understand it, something of a ne'er-do-well, and under circumstances that I do not know, he crossed the Atlantic for the New World a century ago. After a stop in Wisconsin, he headed for southeastern Nebraska, fell in love, and married my grandmother, another member of the rural Swiss community in the farm country outside of Columbus. My grandfather sired six children, including a set of twins, one of whom was my father, born in 1929, just a few months before Black Tuesday and the onset of the Great Depression.

A roughly equal measure of restlessness and a desperation for work during the Depression lured my grandfather west, where he found employment at a paper mill in northern Oregon. He sent money back to support his family for awhile, but soon the letters slowed to a trickle and word filtered east that he wanted a divorce. Back in Nebraska, my father's twin brother had died of pneumonia on a cold winter morning before the twins' first birthday, and when my father's older brother enlisted in the navy a few years later, that left my father as the only son to tend the farm.

Toward the end of his high school years my father and one of his sisters wandered into Columbus one evening to hear a revival preacher who delivered a fiery sermon about God and sin and salvation. My father found Jesus that night, and it changed his life. He returned to the farm determined to dedicate his life to Jesus. A short while later he boarded a train for Chicago, where he enrolled in seminary and met the woman who soon became his wife.

As my father prepared for marriage and for ordination, he vowed never to make the mistakes his father had made. He would serve Jesus singlemindedly, but he would never abandon his wife or his children; he was so determinedly opposed to divorce, in fact, that he resolved never to perform a marriage ceremony for anyone who had been divorced. A promise was a promise—to love, honor, and cherish—and he would always remain true to his word, just as Jesus had been true to his word, even unto death.

The oldest of five sons, I was born before my father completed his seminary studies. I have no real memory of seminary or his first congregation in rural Nebraska, but I know that he threw himself into his work—the days filled with sermon preparations and pastoral visitations, the evenings spent in board and committee meetings. Those commitments multiplied as he became pastor of larger and larger congregations, all of which grew under his stewardship. The Lord's work was demanding, make no mistake about it, and he meant to do it well, to the best of his ability, to do everything to the glory of God.

My father's sons saw him regularly, behind the pulpit every Sunday morning and again on Sunday evening, but the Lord's work left precious little discretionary time for his family. We managed somehow—in the resourceful and resilient way that children do—to fashion our own worlds in the company of one another, friends, jobs, and schoolwork. As products of church and Sunday school ourselves, we understood the importance of his work, and if that meant biking to Little League games by ourselves or not having parents at back-to-school night or missing bat day at Tiger Stadium because it invariably fell on a Sunday, that was okay. Everyone had to make a sacrifice for the Lord. My sacrifice was the presence of my father.

Just a few months before I headed off to college, Harry Chapin released a song called "Cat's in the Cradle," a lament about a father too busy to spend time with his son, who idolizes him: "When ya' coming home, Dad? / I don't know when. / We'll get together then. / You know we'll have a good time then." The lyrics conclude with the father, now retired, asking his son to visit, but the son demurs— "I'd love to, Dad, if I can find the time. / You see, the new job's a hassle and the kids got the flu, / but it's sure nice talking to you."

And in the closing words the father realizes that his son had "grown up just like me. / My boy was just like me."

I heard that song again and again over radio station KIOA as I packed my bags for college, and I resolved that I didn't want to repeat my father's mistakes. Someday, when it was time for me to have a family, my children would know their father. They might love him or hate him—or both—but they would not grow up with an absentee father.

As I headed off to college and began taking all too seriously the task of late adolescence, I developed another resolve: I would never shove my faith down my children's throats like my parents had done to me. I developed a resentment for having grown up as an outsider, someone who, as a preacher's kid, was never part of the "in" group at school, never allowed to participate in dances or social life outside of the church youth group. I came to resent all of the hours I thought I had wasted at youth group gatherings, at vacation Bible school, at Bible camp, at Wednesday evening prayer meetings and Sunday evening services and Sunday school learning stupid songs like "Rolled Away" and "Heavenly Sunshine" and "Zacchaeus Was a Wee Little Man."

As I raged against my evangelical past and all of the indignities I had suffered for the sake of the gospel, for the sake of my father's chosen profession, I resolved that I would never inflict that piety on my sons. Yes, I wanted them to know Jesus, but they should come to Jesus in their own time, in their own way, and not because I stuffed it in their faces. No, I would certainly not make the mistakes my father had made.

Just as I had been born as my father finished seminary, Christian, my first son, was born during my final year of doctoral studies. We lived on the campus of Princeton University at the time; I had my dissertation well in hand, so I spent many hours pushing him around campus in the stroller. He attended his first football game when he was only a few weeks old—a game against

Dartmouth on a cold, blustery November afternoon. He didn't cheer much because he was sleeping snugly in a harness beneath my coat.

Before his first birthday we had moved to Manhattan, of all places, where I began the process of defying the odds against winning tenure at an Ivy League university. Despite the pressures to "publish or perish," one of the perquisites of academic life is the relative freedom to determine your own schedule, so I carefully segregated my classes and meetings into the mornings, Monday through Thursday, when someone could come to the apartment to care for Christian while his mother was away at work. I'd return home at one o'clock on those days to spend the afternoons with my son, hoping that at least a brief afternoon nap would give me an hour or so to begin preparations for the next day's classes, preparations that would resume after multiple readings of *Train Song* and *Goodnight Moon* and a hundred other books had serenaded him to sleep.

Friday, unencumbered by classes or meetings, was our special day. After breakfast and seeing Mom off to work, Christian and I would embark on an adventure. We'd take the subway to South Street Seaport or the Bronx Zoo. We'd visit the Cloisters or take the measure of the vast and bewildering city from atop the Empire State Building. We boarded the M4 bus to the Metropolitan Museum of Art to visit the armor exhibit and the American wing, have lunch, and then take the M4 back home. The planetarium, the moose dioramas, and the huge model of the blue whale lazing eerily above the cafeteria at the Museum of Natural History were perennial favorites. Sometimes on rainy Fridays we would stay home and play with the wooden railroad or build Lego skyscrapers on the dining-room table. By that time, Andrew, my younger son, would join us, making his own contributions.

One Friday, when he must have been about five years old, Christian decided that he wanted to learn how to sing the national anthem. I'm old enough to attest that Vietnam and Richard Nixon pretty much knocked most of the stuffing out of whatever patriotism I once possessed, but how could I deny his request? I have a vivid mental image of the three of us—Christian, Andrew, and me—walking the sidewalks of Morningside Heights singing *The Star-Spangled Banner* at the top of our lungs—over and over again.

On another Friday we had a particular mission, one related to his passion for animals and his continuing frustration that we couldn't have a pet in our crowded New York apartment. Christian climbed onto my lap while I was at the computer that morning and asked my help in composing a leaflet. Those were the early days of computer graphics, but we came up with a line drawing of a baby duckling, and he supplied the text:

Please read!
If you spot a lost animal or a
animal that you can no longer
take care of please return
to 90 morning side drive 10027
(212) 666–0275
We are open weekdays 7:25 am–4pm
weekends 24 hours a day
unless on vacation.
Thank you!

Christian then insisted that we print out a couple of dozen copies. Our task for the day would be to post these notices on bus stop shelters throughout the neighborhood. And we did, discussing in some detail how we would respond when someone called about a bird with a broken wing.

There was little time for church or Sunday school in those days. Sunday was a day of rest, after all, and at the end of an exhausting week of diapers, naps, laundry, grocery-shopping, classes, late-night class preparations, meetings, and maybe a bit of writing, I was ready to collapse. I made a couple of desultory attempts to find a church, but the prospects were so dismal that I gave up, only to try again a few months later and give up again—an endless cycle, it seemed. Besides, I reasoned in my naiveté, I had vowed not to indoctrinate my sons in the way that I had been indoctrinated; surely they would learn about Jesus from the way I talked to them about Jesus and just from watching me in my attempts to be a good person and, more important, a good and attentive and loving father.

Despite the existence of a book by that title, there is no such thing as a "good divorce." Divorce tears at the entire fabric of your being and tests the endurance of everyone involved. The real tragedy of divorce, however, is the collateral damage it inflicts on innocent bystanders, like a cyclone roaring through a sleepy and unsuspecting neighborhood. As a survivor of divorce, I can tell you that neither party is blameless; there is plenty of blame to go around, and I accept more than my share. I can also attest—and I'll try to state this without bitterness—that the laws and the mores of the culture still refuse to countenance the possibility that the father, not the mother, might be the primary caregiver.

I regard it as one of the ironic and mysterious dispensations of grace that, somewhere amid an excruciating divorce that lasted more than five years, I rediscovered, I reconnected with Jesus. Although this was not quite the Jesus I had met in Sunday school—not nearly so invincible or triumphant—I came to rely on this friend closer than a brother, the man of sorrows acquainted with grief. And I came to love him. I loved him fiercely.

My life today is rich and full and happy. I married a wonderful woman who loves Jesus as much as I do. Perhaps more. I have been blessed far more than I deserve. I made my peace with my father in the months before his passing. The cancer advanced so quickly, however, that he never was able to make good on his promise to marry Catharine and me. It would have been the first and only wedding of two divorced people that he had performed in four decades as a minister.

I pray for my sons daily, but I get to see them only once every couple of weeks. I miss our afternoons together and especially our Fridays. I miss seeing them across the dinner table and tucking them into bed at night. I wish I could play catch with Andrew every evening, not just once a fortnight.

My sons spend most of their days now in a household where, I'm fairly certain, the name of Jesus is never spoken—except perhaps as an oath. It weighs heavily on my conscience that Christian and Andrew can't recite the books of the Bible and don't know the words and the motions to "Zacchaeus was a wee little man, and a wee little man was he." I don't know what scars they will carry with them throughout their lives because of my shortcomings. "The sins of the fathers," the book of Deuteronomy declares, "are visited upon the children."

Because of my own manifold failures as a father, I have to rely once again on Jesus. I pray for my sons daily. Sweet Jesus, shield them from the sins of their father. Walk with them when I cannot. Provide comfort and hope and healing. Somewhere out there, dear Jesus, is a bird with a broken wing. Guide him safely home.

# PART 2

# FAMILY MATTERS

I'm a Baptist like my daddy
And Jesus knows my name.

MARY-CHAPIN CARPENTER

# SEARCHING FOR GRANDPA

My grandfather died at the age of ninety-two, but I recall seeing him only twice, perhaps three times, in my life. The reason, I had been led to understand when I was younger, was that he lived too far away, and indeed Oregon did seem like the other end of creation to a child growing up hard by Saginaw Bay. My father's denominational conference was in Seattle one summer, so we swung by to spend a couple of days at my grandfather's farm near Hillsboro, Oregon, outside of Portland. I returned there by myself several years later on my way to a college extension program in southern Oregon.

The memories I have, then, are brief, but they are also vivid, preserved now in the sepia tones of childhood recollection. I remember picking buckets of strawberries in a local field and bing cherries from the heavily laden trees in Grandpa's front yard. He bought my brother and me a softball and bat, and we played for hours in his driveway. What I remember best, I think, is the bucolic setting of his tiny gentleman's farm nestled in the Oregon hills. The rural community in which he lived was called Helvetia and dubbed "Little Switzerland," both, I think, for its concentration of Swiss descendants and for the breathtaking panoramas that do indeed look like parts of Switzerland.

When I returned alone in the mid-seventies, the experience was quite different, and in retrospect I think Grandpa felt a good bit more relaxed and less inhibited when my father was not around. Grandpa drove me in his 1965 Mustang to the Oregon coast, where we sat wordlessly for a long while taking in its incomparable beauty. Along the way he turned to spit tobacco juice out the window, but he had neglected to roll it down. Thinking I hadn't noticed, he discreetly wiped it with a handkerchief, stealing a glance in my direction. We shoveled manure from a local farm into the back of his pickup truck for redistribution in his garden, and when we came in from our chores he offered me some homemade elderberry wine. He also took me by the Helvetia Tavern down the road, where he proudly introduced me to his friends.

After that visit I made the mistake of reporting to my father that Grandpa seemed like a contented and peaceful man, whereupon my father rejoined that he had no right to contentment. It was then that I began to piece together the events of my grandfather's life from the elliptical comments I had heard from family members.

Grandpa was the black sheep of his family, which may account both for his emigration from Switzerland around the turn of the century and for my own affinity with him. He married and settled a homestead in Nebraska, but in the midst of the Depression he headed west in search of work. He eventually found a job in a paper mill and sent money back to Nebraska to support his five children, of whom my father, born in 1929, was the youngest. After a time, however, the money trickled to a halt, and my grandfather never returned to Nebraska. He divorced my grandmother and married a woman in Oregon. Eventually he quit his job in the paper mill in Newburg and resettled in Helvetia, near Hillsboro, where he did odd jobs as the community handyman.

My father never forgave his father for deserting the family and for leaving him back in Nebraska, toiling summer after parched summer. Throughout a pastoral career that spanned forty years, my father never flagged in his unconditional opposition to divorce. He insisted that his position was grounded in Scripture, and perhaps it is, but I think I now understand the real reason for his uncompromising views on the issue.

My father was characteristically reticent when he called a few years back to say that Grandpa had passed away and that he was flying out to Oregon to conduct the funeral. I recall wondering at the time if this might be an important juncture in his life, if he might finally come to terms with his father's treachery and reach some sort of closure on a matter that had plagued him for, well, for a nearly half a century. I called a couple of days after his scheduled return, hoping expectantly for some important disclosure, but all my father could talk about was witnessing to the passenger next to him on the plane ride home.

My travels took me to Portland not long ago, so I took an afternoon away from my work and headed toward Hillsboro, armed only with a vague recollection of the Sunset Highway and a mental image of the Helvetia Tavern. Suburban sprawl has infected the area, and I was several miles off of the highway before the BMWs finally gave way to pickup trucks. A bit farther along, the road curved and suddenly, on the far side of a railroad trestle, the Helvetia Tavern came into view. My grandfather had never been much of a churchman—which, of course, was one of my father's plaints against him—but I remembered that my father had located a plot in the neighborhood churchyard, which couldn't be too far away. I drove past the tavern and wound up the road to a tiny clapboard church. On a hunch, I parked along the side of the road and began to scan the cemetery, which overlooked a broad valley.

Then suddenly, way toward the back, I came across the marker: FRED J. BALMER, 1890–1983. The shock of recognition stunned me momentarily, like a blow to the forehead with a two-by-four. The enigmatic man who had been my grandfather, whose passions had kept him in Oregon even when his responsibilities beckoned half a continent away, now lay beneath the Oregon soil next to the body of his beloved. I, of course, had no way of knowing his disposition when he died, but I was prepared to stand by my earlier assessment. Here was a man who died at peace with himself—aware, certainly, of his own failings and of the adversity and pain his choices had inflicted on others so long ago—but at peace, ultimately, with himself.

After knocking on a couple of doors, I finally found an old-timer in the neighborhood who remembered Grandpa. "Oh yeah," he said, "we threw back a couple of beers together. Your grandfather was quite a character." He looked off toward the distant mountains and then toward my grandfather's farmyard—once meticulous and now dilapidated. "Fred went dancing the night before he died," he continued, thereby providing me with a bit of intelligence my father never divulged. "He passed away the following morning in his easy chair while reading the newspaper." He cleared his throat. "I suppose if you gotta go, that's the way to do it," he said.

Before heading back to the city I stopped at the Helvetia Tavern, its wooden floorboards still smelling of dust the way I had remembered it. They didn't have elderberry wine, so I ordered a Ranier draft and lifted my glass to Grandpa. My father, a teetotaler, would have disapproved of both the gesture and the sentiment.

Grandpa, I think, would have appreciated it.

# POSTCARDS

You don't want those old postcards, do you?" The words, coming from the woman who is now my ex-wife, ostensibly formed a question, but her tone was both plaintive and accusatory at the same time. Over the course of a fifteen-year marriage I'd come to recognize this line of inquiry, as in, "You're not planning another *bike trip*, are you?" Or: "Do you really intend to wear that shirt?" The words only *appear* to form a question; there was, as I understood full well, only one correct and acceptable answer to the postcard question. No, I said obligingly, sensitive to the limitations of space in a New York apartment. Collecting postcards had been a childhood fetish of mine, and three shoeboxes stuffed with photographs of Multnomah Falls and the Grand Canyon and forlorn motel courtyards had followed me all of my adult life.

I reconsidered my answer, however, and muttered a couple of lame rationalizations as I hoisted the three shoeboxes defiantly onto the top shelf of the hall closet. "Some of those old stamps might be worth something," I said unconvincingly. "I'll sort through them soon." (I didn't even persuade myself with that latter statement.)

Then, just last week, I had occasion to haul them down. I needed some help visualizing small towns of the Midwest thirty and forty years ago. I paged through back issues of *Nebraskaland* magazine; I sifted through childhood memories of Nebraska, Iowa, and southern Minnesota, but I still sought more detail.

Aha! The postcards. Three boxes of picture postcards provided the detail I was seeking, but they also opened a window into another world. Most of the cards in my collection date to the middle decades of the twentieth century—the forties, fifties, and sixties—before Instamatic cameras made us a nation of shutterbugs and before interstate highways, television, and fast food obliterated regional distinctions and transformed American culture into something as bland and sterile as a Big Mac. In those days people didn't *drive* across the country; the very term suggests obsession and intensity. Rather, they *motored* from one place to another, and you had the impression that they didn't care very much when they arrived at their destinations or how many stops they made along the way. For a generation just becoming acquainted with the automobile, the destination mattered less than the journey itself.

Indeed, judging from my collection (organized according to state—an early, telltale sign of compulsiveness), there was much to observe along the way. "Pennsylvania is sure full of hills & trees," one correspondent wrote in 1964. "The scenery is beyond explanation," said another. Pilgrims traveling through South Dakota were obliged to stop at Wall Drug, the Corn Palace in Mitchell, and Mount Rushmore in the Black Hills. Who could resist the golden dome of the state capitol in Des Moines or Mark Twain's birthplace in Hannibal, Missouri? And, of course, anyone within a six-hundred-mile radius felt the magnetic pull of Niagara Falls.

Many of the postcards of the forties and fifties celebrated not natural beauty so much as technological prowess. The Pennsylvania Turnpike must have sold thousands of cards, judging by the number in my collection. A card posted in 1954 depicts the "Tulsa Entrance to the Turner Turnpike, Tulsa, Oklahoma." The printed text on the back of the card reads: "The fabulous new Turner Turn-pike was completed at a cost of over $38,000,000. It has reduced the driving distance between Tulsa and Oklahoma City to 88 unimpeded miles." With such a breathless description, no exclamation point was needed.

The skyscrapers of New York, of course, have inspired awe in millions of tourists. "Here we are on the Empire State Building," my father exulted to the folks back home in Nebraska. "Sure a beautiful sight. We really are high." Here's a card of the Union Pacific Railroad bridge in Columbus, Nebraska, and two of the dam at Lake McConaughy out near Ogallala. I confess to a visceral dislike for dams—they seem dark and foreboding to me—but in the 1950s dams and highways and bridges represented progress, the triumph of technology over nature.

The staccato prose on the back of the postcards was brief and almost formulaic: "Fishing was real good. On our way home now." One correspondent, identified only as Adeline, apparently carried a rubber stamp and ink pad on her peregrinations. On the back of a postcard from Washington, D.C., she scratched a few lines ("How have you been? . . . Sure is beautiful!") and then pulled out her rubber stamp for the closing:

*Having a wonderful time,*
*wish you were here.*
*ADELINE*

Writers routinely dispensed with pronouns and articles in order to conserve precious space: "On way home will be home on wk end or maybe even Mon." Even punctuation was sometimes a luxury. "Am in Atlantic City for a few days and am having a swell time will write a letter later and tell you all about it," one card read.

Travelers reported on the weather, the progress of their journeys, or changes in their itineraries. "We had variety of weather—hail, rain,

89

fog," a postcard from the Western Skies Motor Inn in Dalhart, Texas, read. "Dear Mama," my uncle wrote to my grandmother, "We stayed in St. Louis last nite, the roads are fair." "Made it this far yesterday," my aunt wrote on the back of a postcard from the Stardust Motel in Eldorado, Kansas. "Should be there by noon." "There" wasn't specified, but distances didn't seem to matter. "We made pretty good time today but stopped early," a postcard from Marshall, Indiana, reported. "We are just taking our time this trip." "It's only a little over 300 miles to Howard's folks," a card from the Motel Vagabond in Wheatland, Indiana, explained, "so decided we'd better go see them too since we're so close."

Restaurant and diner food along the way was uneven and, for my family at least, an extravagance. It was simpler to pack a lunch, and stopping to eat at some park provided the occasion to scrawl a note on the back of a postcard. "We are at Fort Dodge now and have come about 300 miles," my father, newly married, reported to his mother back in Nebraska. "The lunch is wonderful, especially the chicken." "Homeward bound and just stopped off here to eat some sandwiches that Nancy made for us," one correspondent wrote from Arnold's Park, Iowa. Frugality on the road became a kind of game. "We have a car icebox full of food, so we have been eating something about every hour," my mother noted somewhere in Ohio. "Thanks a lot for everything," my grandmother wrote at the conclusion of her bus trip from Bay City, Michigan, to Columbus, Nebraska. "The lunch lasted till home. Just got off and got 1 cup of coffee at Des Moines, Iowa."

The long stretches between one place and another allowed travelers to fret about things at home—water in the basement or the house burning down. Postcards provided a succinct way to sound a warning and to ease a troubled mind. "Are you having very bad weather?" someone far from home asked. "I just think you have and it worries me." "Dear Clarence," my grandmother wrote to my father on December 18, 1941, "I wish you would not light the candles on the tree too much." And, a decade later, my father, off at college,

90

reciprocated his concern. "How's everything back home?" he asked. "Do you have enough wood to burn?"

A postcard very often conveyed reassurance. "Just a card to let you know we are fine & hope you are alright too," my aunt wrote from Gene Autry, Oklahoma. "The weather is fine & we're enjoying our trip," my mother reported on the back of an aerial view of the Pennsylvania Turnpike. "We won't be driving after dark."

People who wrote postcards were guileless; they had nothing to hide. Anyone could—and probably did—read the sentiments on a postcard, but the writer seemed to understand that. A postcard was no place for secrets. It did, however, provide an opportunity for a quick apology or the promise of a letter to follow. "Will write a letter soon," one correspondent said, "I forgot to get some stationery." "I don't have time anymore to write a letter," my father lamented in 1945, "so I'll just write a card." Six years later his life was still busy. "Seems like I don't have time to do much letter writing anymore," he noted on the back of a picture of Chicago's Outer Drive. "I'll try to write a letter soon."

In a few instances the provenance of the card helped to explain lapses in communication. "Sorry I've not written more," my aunt apologized on the back of an aerial view of Guthrie, Oklahoma, "but not much to write about all the time." Sometimes a postcard was a plaintive appeal for news—"I sure would like to hear from some one back home" and "I was rather expecting to hear from you today," or it provided a tease about more news to follow. "I'll have some newsy news for you in my next letter," my aunt promised in 1944. "Good news. Wait & see."

We don't send postcards very often anymore, much less letters. The revolution in communications technology over the past quarter-century has transformed us into a nation of talkers—talk radio, talk television, CB radios, cellular telephones. Sitting down to write a letter, even a postcard, requires thought and reflection, an expenditure of time and effort we are no more prepared to make than we are willing to spend an extra hour or two traveling U.S. 30 rather than Interstate 80. Whereas conversation prizes spontaneity, correspondence demands at least a measure of clarity and perspicuity. It's much easier to pick up a telephone and blurt out whatever comes to mind.

My grandmother gave me most of the postcards in my collection. As mother of five children, she served as the vortex on a compass as her children and grandchildren ventured out in every direction—Pennsylvania, Michigan, Oregon, New Mexico. They all stayed in touch, however, through postcards.

Grandma now spends her days and nights at a nursing home in Nebraska. I don't write to her as often as I should, in part because I don't have enough to say that would fill up an entire letter.

Perhaps she'd appreciate a postcard.

# MY FATHER'S CARS

M y father has never overcome his childhood fascination with the automobile. He is not a man who dwells on the hardships of the past, so when he talks about growing up the conversation often veers toward his first automobile, purchased in the early forties for the impossible sum of sixty dollars.

I'm sure I cannot fathom all that a 1929 Model A Ford symbolized to a poor farmboy, but it almost certainly represented a means of escaping the dust and drudgery of farm work, even for a few hours. Friday-night trips into town opened the window to a world that looked increasingly enticing and engendered in him a restlessness and a thirst for travel that even the passing years have not quenched.

As it turned out, a call from God, not a carburetor, liberated him from the Nebraska soil. In the early fifties he headed for seminary in Chicago, a city just then waking to the pleasures of motoring. The woman who became his wife and my mother had many attractive and endearing qualities to engage the attentions of an earnest seminarian, but not least among them, I'm sure, was her father's late-model Cadillac, and when her suitor proved himself the honorable and trustworthy man that he was, that Cadillac ferried them on romantic excursions throughout the Windy City.

After a honeymoon to Wisconsin and a sojourn in Nebraska, my parents settled into a parish in rural Minnesota. There began a succession of shiny automobiles whose photographs still adorn the pages of family albums. I remember a two-tone Roadmaster, a rust-colored Buick with huge fins, a Pontiac sedan. At some point—it may have been the '63 Chevrolet Impala—my father purchased his first new car, rather than used, and along about the late sixties a growing family and the move to a city made us a two-car family.

Like so many others of his generation, the fifties bred into my father a love for big automobiles, a passion he indulged even through the oil crises of the seventies. I don't believe my father ever seriously regretted his choice of vocation, but I do recall on several occasions the sorrow he felt that he must temper his taste in automobiles in order to suit the expectations of his congregation. When some parishioner would offer a handsome discount on a used Oldsmobile or Continental, my father reluctantly said no, afraid that such ostentation would raise too many eyebrows.

My father passed his love for automobiles on to his sons, three of whom have worked for car dealers. At early ages we learned to spot Buick LeSabres or Ford Galaxies at a considerable distance, and we peered over his shoulder to remind him that the speedometer was creeping past seventy or wonder if the gas gauge wasn't perilously low. Every fall, whether my father happened to be in the market for a car or not, we'd make the rounds of the car dealers to check out the new models and argue their relative merits. Sixteenth birthdays were rites of passage, complete with an early morning visit to the driver's examiner, a duplicate set of car keys, and the obligatory photograph of the initiate behind the wheel, his left elbow poking out the window in a gesture of studied insouciance.

In our family, when other topics of conversation seemed dicey—especially during the years of impasse that afflict fathers and their late-adolescent sons—the talk turned to automobiles. When I'd come home from college one of my father's first questions was always, "How'd the car run?" Or, "What are gas prices out your way?" Hastily, I'd have to reconstruct what I'd paid for fuel in the next county or the next state because shaving a couple of cents off a gallon of gasoline was always important for an aficionado like my father, a practice he's continued in recent years not so much out of economic stringency as for the mere sport of it.

Not long ago my father phoned to say that he'd purchased a sporty, imported van for a vacation trip to the Pacific Northwest. He's reached the age and the financial status now where he can afford to indulge some of his whims. I'm not sure how long he'll be satisfied with this new automobile before something else captures his imagination, but that something else almost certainly will be a car.

# THE PASSING OF AN ERA

M y grandmother passed away just a year and three months shy of her one hundredth birthday.

She was born in a log cabin on a homestead in the sandhill country of southeastern Nebraska, an area settled by Swiss-Germans. She never lived more than fifteen miles from her birthplace, yet she had seen some remarkable changes over the course of the twentieth century. The Soviet Union rose and fell within her lifetime. Her parents had lived in sod huts near the Loup River, and Grandma lived long enough to sit in her living room chair and watch a man walk on the moon.

Not that she did much sitting. Grandma worked hard all of her life, yet she never knew riches. My grandfather left to find work during the Great Depression, and he never returned. Grandma was left to rear six children on a hundred-acre farm outside of Columbus, working tirelessly to provide for her family.

It was never easy—the sweltering sun, the disappointing harvests, the bitter winters. During the Dust Bowl years the soil would blow furiously, filling shoes and kitchens and ditches. Before the

97

widespread use of irrigation in the 1960s, drought—sometimes two years out of three—would cause the crops to emerge stillborn from the soil. My father and his sisters recall harvesting ears of corn no larger than pine cones.

Then the personal tragedies. My father's twin brother died of pneumonia before his first birthday. Grandma carried that grief to her grave, yet somehow she persevered, year after year, winter after winter, season after season.

Above all, she loved the land. She planted gardens and a small orchard; nothing delighted her so much as the sound of songbirds. So tidy was her farmstead that she would patrol the grounds several times a day tugging on the odd weed, gathering twigs and chicken feathers in her apron.

When her children finally prevailed upon her to move into town in 1962, where she spent the final third of her life, I think she felt lost and overwhelmed. She planted a huge garden that overtook the entire back yard, and she found solace there amid the lilacs, tomatoes, and zinnias.

I never knew her before her hands were gnarled from work. She always walked hunched over from having pulled out so many weeds over the course of a lifetime. Whenever we visited her in Columbus she insisted on driving out to the farm to have another look and, I think, to mourn silently at the dishevelment of the place.

Not many farmsteads are left in the countryside where Grandma spent most of her ninety-eight years. The farmhouse itself is old and dilapidated and uncared-for. The huge red barn, once the showplace of the entire community, recently collapsed beneath the ravages of time and neglect. Grandma's death marks the passing of an era. All of her children have opted out of farming, and there is no one left to carry on the tradition. Grandma's farm will go on the market soon and be sold to the highest bidder.

Dust to dust.

On the morning after the funeral, her children gathered at the cemetery—not by prearrangement; it was some kind of homing instinct, I think. They walked through the tiny churchyard behind the church where they had all taken their confirmation classes, and they reminisced about the names on the stones and about times past. The "free shows" in nearby Duncan, when silent movies came to the town square. The sound of the whistle from the steam loco-motives on the Union Pacific Railroad, so near yet so far away. The wonders of Franklin Roosevelt's New Deal, which brought shelter breaks to the fields, cement-enclosed privies to the schoolyard, and, miracle of miracles, electricity to the farmhouses. My father and his sisters walked back and forth through the churchyard. Here lay their own grandparents and Aunt Ella and Heck Blaser and over there a plot of bachelor farmers. The tiny gravestone of my father's twin brother has held up well over the last sixty-five years.

My father insisted that Grandma's faith grew significantly in her later years. Her Bible was well-thumbed, and toward the end of her life, as her short-term memory faded, she often prayed in Schweiz-Deutsch (Swiss-German).

My grandmother was laid to rest on a Tuesday afternoon on a small rise in the Gruetli Cemetery. She faces the farmstead just down the road, clearly visible across the flat Nebraska prairie.

I think I heard songbirds.

# SOME THOUGHTS ON ATTENDING A FIFTEEN-YEAR COLLEGE REUNION

From the perspective of fifteen years, I can now divide my college experience into two fairly distinct phases. I remember well the anxiety of pulling into the parking lot at a small evangelical college in the suburbs of Chicago, feeling both anticipation and apprehension about what lay before me. I found the spartan and ramshackle campus comforting somehow. There was a kind of makeshift quality to it that seemed familiar to someone whose notion of luxury while growing up was a Holiday Inn hotel room. Perhaps I wasn't in over my head, after all.

I was unprepared for the warmth and acceptance that enveloped me in the ensuing days and weeks. For someone reared in a fundamentalist household, who had felt the sting of rejection by his peers, I basked in the warm embrace of the evangelical subculture that I had known only intermittently—on Sundays and Wednesday nights in church or at Bible camp during the summers—through childhood and early adolescence. My classmates at this Christian college looked and dressed like I did, which is to say conservatively with close-cropped hair; they even spoke the same language as me. They talked unabashedly about the Bible, about their private devotions, about their struggle to "know God's will" for their lives. Indeed, God-talk conferred a certain status at this evangelical school. Those who spoke the parlance of evangelical piety most fluently were immediately regarded as leaders. Growing up in a parsonage, I'd had years of practice, so the only logical course was to run for president of my freshman class. I recall wondering at the time at how far I had come in just a few short weeks—from a cipher in high school to a campus leader of sorts in college.

The second phase of my college experience kicked in only gradually. Intoxicated by the acceptance I felt, I allowed my studies to founder. The first "C" in my life, however, got my attention, and I began to recognize that this college, in the early seventies, was indeed an unusual place by the standards of evangelical higher education. The school's president in those years was an engaging and intellectually curious man whose chief virtue was his refusal to pander to the basest instincts of the sectarian, fundamentalist constituency that provided much of the school's support. Gingerly but persistently, he probed the boundaries of acceptability, sometimes at great personal cost to himself and considerable financial cost to the school. He allowed movies (*some* movies, at least) on campus and began to relax some of the parietal rules that governed student life. He tolerated guest lectures by such "radicals" as Jesse Jackson. His most daring move, however, came in the mid-seventies, and everyone understood why, for political reasons, a rousing evening of square dances in the gymnasium had to be called "folk games."

Most important, the president allowed the dean of the college to assemble an extraordinary group of bright, energetic faculty members, most of them fresh out of graduate school. This cohort, all of them reared in evangelical households, took on a murderous regimen of four or five courses a semester and proceeded to challenge the presuppositions of their theologically, politically, and socially conservative students. At least some of those students began

102

for the first time to question the morality of America's involvement in Vietnam, the utility of dispensational premillennialism, or the integrity of middle-class values. Some even let their hair grow long and traded their pressed khakis and monogrammed shirts for the denim rusticity of their mentors.

I shall always be grateful to those professors and, by extension, to the college for providing that environment. The place was far from perfect, but it served for me as a kind of halfway house between the fundamentalism of my childhood and the wider world. I almost didn't attend college at all, but I have often reflected on how my life would be different had I enrolled in a state university instead of a Christian college. I suspect that I would have retreated further into the evangelical subculture, that I would have erected tall barriers against what I had been taught to revile as the alien, godless ideologies of the secular academy. This evangelical college, however, to shift the metaphor, provided a safe harbor for my intellectual dog paddles into the sea of secularism; I was seldom beyond the reach of a life buoy in the hands of someone who was learning to swim the same waters.

I began first by questioning the conservative political views of the subculture, which I came to regard as narrow and self-interested. I became disquieted by evangelical attitudes toward women, which struck me as chauvinist at best, and probably misogynist. In my youthful impetuosity, I came to regard evangelicals' vicious theological controversies as churlish and irrelevant, the intellectual equivalent of shoring up the Maginot Line.

But the subculture, as I learned from bitter experience, does not countenance anyone calling its shibboleths into question, especially one of its own who ought to know better. In retrospect, I should have left earlier than I did, but I was reluctant to trade the familiar comfort of the evangelical cocoon I had known all of my life for the uncertainty of the broader world. My prospects of being accepted for graduate study at Princeton University were roughly equivalent to my chances of winning the Illinois lottery, but graduate school proved infinitely rewarding both for its intellectual challenges and for the camaraderie of faculty and fellow students who introduced me to a Christianity shorn of fundamentalist accoutrements.

I've had little contact with my *alma mater*, but I returned to the Chicago suburbs for my fifteen-year class reunion. The place had changed a great deal since the early seventies. Conservatives among the school's constituency finally succeeded in toppling the president and replacing him with a slick, oleaginous preacher who knows how to pander. The new president quickly purged the remnant of iconoclasts left over from the seventies and returned the college safely to the orbit of sectarianism.

A good number of my classmates applauded the changes, pointing to new buildings, increased enrollments, and the winning record of the football team as indices of improvement over the years. Such tangible signs of prosperity are difficult to gainsay in a culture that measures success by victories, numbers, and buildings, even unsightly, cinder-block structures. But I felt a tragic sense of loss throughout an evening of self-congratulatory speeches and breathless soliloquies about God's faithfulness. I may well be wrong, but I found it difficult to imagine that any but the most resolute rebel would emerge from the college willing to challenge the pretensions and the presuppositions of evangelicalism.

The evangelical subculture, which prizes conformity above all else, will never again recognize me as its own, except for the prodigal that I suppose I am. There was a time when I mourned that, but no longer. While most evangelical prodigals, in my experience, have discarded their faith altogether, the challenge for me since leaving college has been to sift through the cultural baggage of evangelicalism to see if there is anything of value at its core. I think there is: the juxtaposition of the doctrine of depravity with a radical understanding of God's ineluctable grace. The emphasis of one at the expense of the other, in my view, defines the difference between evangelical and liberal in contemporary Protestant theology. Although it's not a popular position these days, I choose to embrace both doctrines simultaneously, in part because I have seen powerful evidence of both depravity and grace in my own life.

The people at my *alma mater* may give lip service to such affirmations, but their notion of grace, I think, is severely attenuated by a legalism dictated by their subculture. That legalism, together with the insistence upon conformity, largely quashes creativity and critical engagement. For many, it also leads to personal despair, as I was reminded in poignant conversations with several classmates who still struggle with feelings of guilt and inadequacy because they cannot affirm the right doctrines or conjure the requisite piety for full acceptance by the subculture.

For a brief, shining moment in its history this tiny, inconsequential liberal arts school stood apart from all that. As chance (or *providence*) would have it, I ran into one of those bright, young professors from the early seventies who had exerted such a formative influence on my life and on the lives of others. He laughed heartily when I revealed that he had given me that chastening "C" back in my first semester of college. Both of us, it turned out, had forged an uneasy peace with evangelicalism, but neither of us felt very comfortable with trappings of the subculture. We drank a toast to the old days and reminisced about absent colleagues, trading intelligence about who was where doing what. Those were exhilarating days, we agreed, in part because of the intellectual ferment on campus, but also because of the sheer titillation of challenging the evangelical establishment.

Inevitably, of course, those challenges had been turned back, for institutions are inherently conservative, and evangelicals have long confused dissent with personal affront. But we were better somehow for having mounted the assault.

# EYES ON THE FENCEPOST

Some Remarks on the Occasion
of Clarence R. Balmer's Retirement
April 12, 1996

---

I t is the farm stories that I remember best, the illustration tucked
neatly into the sermon a few minutes before noon, just as the junior high kids, seated toward the back, were beginning to get restless. My father, having read the text and explained the context,
would reach for some anecdote to demonstrate his point, to give
the folks something to take home to Sunday dinner. Three points
and a poem, they teach you in homiletics class, but a story would
do just as well, maybe better.

I recall stories about new tenants transforming an empty, dirty
apartment and a word or phrase or observation coming out of the
mouths of children. "Kids say the darndest things," as Art Linkletter
used to say. And for a preacher, no doubt, a large family had its advan-
tages when it came time every week to sit before the typewriter and
pound out next Sunday's sermon.

But the farm stories resonated best somehow, pages from a
Depression-era childhood on the plains of Nebraska. You shivered
with him on the long walk to the one-room schoolhouse, stopping
in the corn shocks along the way for shelter from the wind. You felt
the blistering sun in the summer, the dust in your teeth at the end of

107

a long day of planting, cultivating, or harvesting. Even the junior high kids in the back, who wouldn't know a John Deere from a Massey-Ferguson if their skateboards depended on it, suddenly stopped their wiggling to pay attention to the preacher.

My favorite sermon illustration was the one about plowing a straight line. My father would tell how his grandfather abhorred sloppy furrows and how he took his grandson aside one day to reveal the secret of plowing a straight line: "Keep your eyes fixed on a fencepost at the far end of the field," he said. "Don't look right or left, just straight ahead, and your furrow will be straight."

There is something in that story, I think, about grit and determination and perseverance, about refusing to be distracted by vainglory or jealousy or pettiness.

The farmboy from Nebraska learned his lesson well. Fixing his eyes on the far fencepost meant leaving the farm for seminary, where he met and married the woman of his dreams, who became a partner beyond his wildest dreams. In the early years, it meant long hours in the study preparing at least two sermons a week, a radio broadcast, a meditation for Wednesday-night prayer meeting, and a lesson for the adult Sunday school class. It also meant typing the bulletin, cranking the mimeograph machine, and perhaps even dusting the pews in that small country church—and all of that between calls at the hospital twenty miles away.

Eyes on the far fencepost meant forty years of being there to observe the passages of lives—the celebration of birth, countless marriages, illnesses, and graduations, providing comfort and the assurance of resurrection to the grieving.

We are gathered this evening to observe one of those passages in the life of a farmboy from Nebraska who made his mother proud—and his wife and his children. The fencepost at the far end of the field is still in his sights. And if the preacher on this occasion would permit himself a quick glance back over his shoulder, he would see what those of us who love and admire him have known for a long, long time: The furrow he has plowed is straight indeed.

It is very, very straight.

# PART 3

# GLIMPSES OF GRACE

We sleep to time's hurdy-gurdy;
we wake, if we ever awake,
to the silence of God.

ANNIE DILLARD

# CALIFORNIA DREAMIN'

In the American West, image and reality don't always coincide. Nothing is quite what it seems. As Ian Frasier pointed out in a recent series of *New Yorker* articles, Billy the Kid was born Henry McCarty in New York City. Bat Masterson died of a heart attack at his desk, where he spent his last years as a sports columnist for the *New York Morning Telegraph*. The infamous Wyatt Earp died not in a Dodge City gunfight but in Los Angeles. On the other hand, one of the most famous sons of the American West is Robert Frost, who was born in California, although he remains forever associated with the snowy woods of New England.

What calls all of this to mind is a research trip to southern California that doubled as family vacation. No visitor to the Golden Land can fail to be impressed with the diverse and stunning beauty of California—the Big Sur, Point Loma, Laguna Beach, the incomparable Redwoods that have managed somehow to survive lightning and loggers and even James Watt, Ronald Reagan's secretary of the interior. California has a staggering and almost scandalous fecundity. Effortlessly, it seems, the state produces more of just about everything—from almonds to zucchini—than just about everywhere else.

Through the quintessentially California media of celluloid and video, the Golden State has cast its long shadow across the rest of the country. In the sixties and seventies, Detroit named its automobiles after California landmarks—Malibu, Laguna, Monterey. California, with the nation's largest and most diverse economy, gave us Disneyland, the Beach Boys, hot tubs, and wine coolers, not to mention Richard Nixon and Ronald Reagan. As Robert MacNeill has pointed out, California has also augmented the American lexicon with expressions like "groovy," "far out," and, more recently, "gnarly." California must have invented the word "natural" too. Everything is natural, from cotton T-shirts to frozen yogurt. To their eternal credit, all five of California's major league baseball teams—five teams!—play their home games under the sky on natural grass rather than in the polyester stadiums so common in other cities.

Just beneath the veneer of palm trees and prosperity and golden bodies frolicking in the surf, however, image and reality diverge. What should be "the happiest place on earth," to borrow Disneyland's slogan, is slowly choking on its own effluvia. Development has run amok; housing tracts blanket every canyon and hillside in sight. Having long ago used up what little water was available locally, southern California is in the process of draining huge lakes hundreds of miles away and has now cast its jealous eyes on the Colorado River. Orange County, home to Disneyland, is now a tragic misnomer; what was once a fertile valley lined with orange groves and bean fields is now, in effect, a huge parking lot veined with a mishmash of highways that become impassible during daylight hours. California's romanticization of the automobile has left a huge impenetrable cloud the color of dirty dishwater.

It is difficult to see all this and not be overcome by the tragedy of it—the squandered resources, the lost opportunities. It has even become fashionable on the part of some longtime residents (defined roughly as those who moved to California *last* year) to resent the intrusion of newcomers and to pine for the pastel days of the fifties when southern California more nearly resembled a Mediterranean paradise. Such halcyon evocations, however, have little resonance in California, where, as Joan Didion wrote in one of her haunting essays, "The future always looks good in the golden land, because no one remembers the past."

One can easily sermonize about stewardship of God's creation—to whom much has been given, and so forth—but that would be hypocritical coming from a fellow American. Besides, Californians have heard all that before, so I'll spare them another peroration. Californians are just like the rest of us, only more so. We're all guilty of squandering resources, of wasting water and spewing fluorocarbons into the atmosphere.

But the tragedy is somehow more evident here. "Of all the lands I have seen," the peripatetic J. C. Simmons wrote in 1902, "there is none to compare with America, and in America, none to compare with California." Several decades earlier Lorenzo Waugh, a Methodist circuit rider, christened California the new Eden.

The Edenic purity and innocence are gone now, hidden behind a blanket of smog, buried somewhere beneath a shopping mall or one of those cynical developments called Pine Ridge Estates or Pleasant Valley Acres—named for the very natural wonder that it has obliterated. And yet there are occasional glimmers of hope, times when the image again emerges from the dusty shadows of reality. The Santa Ana winds kick up now and again and scour the valley, thereby bringing to naught the best efforts of Angelenos to poison themselves. Down the coast the sea fog burns off by ten o'clock every morning and exposes a crystalline sky. A dry and gentle breeze whispers through the palms. And in the afternoon the sun cuts a million diamonds in the surf before it slides gently into the Pacific.

It's enough to make you believe in grace.

# NEW YORK CITY, GEORGE STEINBRENNER, AND COMMON GRACE

W hen my wife and I and our young son, not yet a year old, moved to New York City, we did so with fear and trepidation, leavened ever so slightly with a spirit of adventure. Living in New York City had never figured into even our wildest imaginings; I had envisioned teaching at a bucolic, small-town college somewhere—Grinnell, perhaps, or Davidson—never in New York. But we were trapped, in a way. Two years and fifty-some applications had netted me two interviews and precisely one job offer—in New York City.

We gave ourselves five years, at the conclusion of which we would almost certainly have other options (especially because I had been assured, in no uncertain terms, that I would never receive tenure at the university where I had been hired). Perhaps if I worked hard enough, exercised the trusty Puritan work ethic, an offer would come from what I sometimes referred to as the "real world" west of the Hudson. In the meantime, we would simply tough it out in New York.

115

Our families, Midwesterners all, thought we had lost our minds, and I recall vividly my father's reaction when I informed him that we had divested ourselves of our automobile a month after moving to Manhattan. "You what?" he shrieked into the phone, trying even so to temper his astonishment. It took me some time, but I managed to persuade him that a car in New York is really an albatross. That divestment remains probably the single most liberating act I have ever undertaken.

We recently began our sixth year in Manhattan. Our apartment looks across the street into Harlem, and just this morning I did what I once believed was unthinkable: I delivered my older son to the kindergarten classroom of a New York City public school. Despite my occasional repugnance at the very notion, New York is beginning to feel like home. I now find it difficult to begin a day without a perusal of the *New York Times*. The visceral energy of New York is, I confess, intoxicating, although I maintain that it's easier to live here than it is to visit. When you live in New York, you can take it in a little at a time rather than contending with the sensory overload that inevitably afflicts tourists.

Visitors, however, generally have the advantage of leaving the city before its patina wears off, because, as any resident knows only too well, New York has more than its share of problems. Car alarms, traffic, general rudeness, drugs, crime, and too many yuppies all diminish the quality of life here. Add to that the scourge of AIDS, official incompetence and corruption, and the day-to-day brutality of life and you have plenty of reasons to steer clear of the Big Apple.

New Yorkers usually confront such indignities with a determined stoicism, but occasionally some event arouses us from our apathetic stupor and prompts us to take stock of ourselves and our city. The vigilante-type subway shootings by Bernhard Goetz several years ago was one such event, as were the Howard Beach and the Bensonhurst killings. Equally jarring was the brutal rape of a young woman who became known popularly as the Central Park jogger. Another catalyst for self-appraisal on the part of New Yorkers was the slaying in the subway of a young tourist from Utah, who was trying to protect his mother from a gang of would-be muggers.

The incident outraged New Yorkers, who, appearances notwithstanding, can be inordinately sensitive about how we are perceived by "outsiders." The tabloids covered the story obsessively, to the point of dispatching reporters to Utah to interview the victim's neighbors. Editorials called on the mayor to express his outrage in what would be, presumably, a catharsis for the entire city. The governor chimed in with the promise of more police officers.

Such moments of indignation occur all too rarely in New York City. We put up with far too much before our rage boils over in righteous anger. And yet, like the famous Peace Corps advertisement that asked if the glass was half empty or half full, we need a sense of perspective in times of crisis. The stabbing of the young man from Utah was undeniably tragic, craven, and senseless, but something like three and a half million people ride the subways every day, and the incidence of crime, given those numbers, is remarkably small. Ugly racial tensions flare much too frequently, and an occasional violent event catapults the issue into public consciousness, but in fact we New Yorkers get along surprisingly well; a heterogeneous environment such as this demands accommodation and understanding. Most New Yorkers appreciate the city's rich ethnic and racial pastiche. My son's three best friends in nursery school were, respectively, African-American, Asian, and Jewish. I don't think that would have happened in Davidson, North Carolina.

What makes New York work as well as it does? What keeps this city from erupting in a conflagration of hatred and violence? John Calvin, I think, would attribute it to common grace, and I honestly cannot come up with a better explanation. I am not naive enough about the human condition to suppose that New York City will ever be Eden, but clinging to the doctrine of grace allows me to hope that we will maintain a semblance of comity, that we will somehow avoid destroying one another. Some days I even dare to hope that, with enlightened political leadership, a little help from Washington, and a generous measure of that grace, we might even be able provide homes for the wretched men who sleep on park benches across the street from my bedroom window.

It's not likely, perhaps, at least not anytime soon. But the corollary of grace, even common grace, is hope. George Steinbrenner, after all, was once banished from baseball. Can redemption be far behind?

# ORANGE COUNTY JOURNAL

———

he future always looks good in the golden land," Joan Didion
wrote in one of her piercing essays about California, "because
no one remembers the past." Indeed, ahistoricism seems to be
a way of life here in southern California. How else do you account
for Hollywood's disregard of historical verity in movies like *Mississippi Burning* or in desultory attempts by Sylvester Stallone and
Chuck Norris to write revisionist histories of the Vietnam War? My
fourteenth-floor hotel room in Orange County looks out over a
huge housing development that covers several square miles. The
architecture is identical throughout, a sea of red tile roofs in the
ersatz mission style so popular in southern California, evoking a
romantic past that has been all but obliterated by—well, by housing tracts such as this.

Hard by the development is a deep sluiceway, but the raging
waters that once filled its banks have been reduced to a trickle, testimony to Orange County's insatiable appetite for water. As a historian of the American West once told me, southern California has
no right to exist at all. Indeed, every patch of green, every palm

tree and bougainvillea blossom, is artificial, having been coaxed out of the ground by water pilfered from sources hundreds of miles away. I wonder if anyone here has paused to consider that if the tap suddenly ran dry—as doomsayers insist that it will—Orange County itself would dry up and blow away. Southern California would then become the new dust bowl; the very descendants of the Okies who fled the Dust Bowl of the thirties will have helped to create a second.

So much for the lessons of history. The denizens of Orange County, careening from one oil crisis to the next in air-conditioned comfort, seem blissfully unperturbed by such ruminations. They just don't seem to get it, intent as they are on pursuing the California dream of fast, shiny cars, limitless affluence, and sybaritic leisure. That relatively few seem to attain the dream doesn't deter them; the vision itself, endlessly reiterated in video and celluloid, is so compelling that thousands arrive annually to join the quest. Newly released census figures, albeit preliminary, indicate that California's population has increased by thirty-some percent in the last decade.

If Didion is correct that no one here remembers the past, that precludes the possibility of learning from the past. This, I discovered, applies on a personal level as well. In the course of interviewing high school students from a large evangelical church here in Orange County, I asked about the youth culture of southern California. What was it like to be a teenager in Fullerton or Costa Mesa or Newport Beach? The answers were probably not all that different from those that might come from high school students in other parts of the country, but I found the portrayal exceedingly grim. "The main goal is to fit in," one said. Teenagers in Orange County grope for an identity in activities and interests dictated by their peer groups, which in turn are defined by ethnic background, fashion, or musical tastes. The jocks hang out with the cheerleaders. Beach people stick together. Heavy metal devotees or rappers stay with their own ilk. The portrait that emerged was one of an atomistic culture that breeds insecurity, dissolution, and aimlessness.

"They seem like they're happy on the outside," one man said, "but they're so empty."

A woman in the group then volunteered an illustration that has haunted me ever since I heard it. She told of an acquaintance in high school who, to all appearances, had it all. She was intelligent, good-looking, and a cheerleader, the very pinnacle of popularity. But something, somewhere, went awry. The dream apparently turned to desolation, and she committed suicide. The young woman's parents, however, didn't get it. Even their daughter's tragic gesture failed to command their attention: They had her buried in her cheerleader's uniform.

I don't know the details of this woman's life, what private anguish drove her to her desperate act, but the poignancy of her story brings me to the verge of tears. I don't know her parents, but, in some small way, I share in their grief. At the same time, I wonder if there isn't something to be learned from a young woman whose body moulders in an Orange County grave—in a cheerleading outfit.

# REMEMBERING JOHN LENNON

The anniversary, I confess, had slipped my mind entirely. Only midway through a bicycle ride around Central Park on a Sunday afternoon did I notice a congregation of the faithful gathered at Strawberry Fields.

They had come to remember John Lennon who, eleven years earlier, on December 8, 1980, had been gunned down outside his apartment at the Dakota, just across Central Park West on 72nd Street. They brought roses and candles and notes and incense and placed them carefully on the circular "Imagine" mosaic that has become Lennon's most visible memorial. Someone, for some reason, contributed a dog-eared copy of *Crime and Punishment*. "We miss you, John," one sign read. Another, simply, "Thanks, John." Beneath the gray December sky, many sat cross-legged on the ground, staring at the mosaic, lost in reverie.

Lennon, I think, would have been pleased at the congregation— and perhaps a bit amused. Those in attendance reflected the various stages of his own life. Some wore the trademark wire-rimmed glasses. Others had taken on the more refined look of Lennon's later years. One middle-aged man with black bangs and a bowl haircut had even managed to shoehorn himself into a "Beatle suit" from the "I Wanna Hold Your Hand" years, the gray coat without lapels, accented with black piping. And there were hippies, people with tired eyes and worn faces who, without muttering a word, told you more than you cared to know about the ravages of alcohol, drugs, and deflated ideals.

They remembered with candles, incense, and notes, but most of all they remembered with music. One group, strumming imaginary guitars, huddled around a boom box, another sang *a capella*: "Strawberry Fields Forever," "Nowhere Man," "Let It Be," and, of course, "Imagine."

When the news of his assassination spread a decade ago, radio stations played Lennon's song "In My Life," which began, "There are places I remember in my life, though some have changed," and I recall being overcome by an ineffable sadness. Sadness at Lennon's death, to be sure, but also because I was reminded of the places and the people in my own past that I could never recover. I mourned the loss of an innocence that, in ways I don't fully understand, was shaped by Lennon and his music. Like many others of my generation who grew up in fundamentalist households, Lennon and the Beatles were strictly off limits. The young Liverpudlians were brash and defiant; they represented everything that our parents, who had come of age in the soporific fifties, feared. Even in their early years, you had the sense that Lennon and company understood that something was terribly wrong with Western culture—its materialism, its vapid religion, its easy resort to violence.

But our parents' objections didn't deter us. We grew up with John Lennon or, rather, we followed him, because he always seemed to be a step or two ahead of everyone else, from his experimentation with Yoga and Transcendental Meditation to his opposition to the Vietnam War. The former chorister at St. Peter's Church, Woolton, was always a visionary, but his musings in later years took on a utopian cast. He asked us to give peace a chance, and in the spare, haunting melody of his most famous song, he invited us to imagine no heaven or hell, no fighting or violence, no nations, people simply living for today.

The Calvinist in me, which still refuses to die, scoffed at such simple-mindedness. Such a world could never exist, I reasoned, and Lennon's own death at the hands of a deranged gunman seemed to vindicate the redoubtable theologian from Geneva.

Still, I wonder if we have dismissed Lennon too blithely. Even John Calvin believed in common grace, the notion that we can live together in a measure of peace, despite our wretchedness. It is a fragile and imperfect foundation, to be sure, but one that perhaps, to paraphrase Lennon, deserves a chance.

Lennon understood better than most that one generation, in contemplating its own failures, invests its hopes in the next. Not long ago my seven-year-old son and I visited Strawberry Fields in Central Park. We came upon the "Imagine" mosaic, and I explained the nature of the memorial. When he asked what was so extraordinary about John Lennon I found myself, uncharacteristically, at a loss for words. He was a man who thought that people ought to be able to get along with one another, I said finally, that nations shouldn't hurl bombs at one another, that people shouldn't hurt one another.

My seven-year-old found nothing extraordinary about that whatsoever.

# SILICON VALLEY

W hen I first heard the term *Silicon Valley* more than a decade ago, I thought it had something to do with artificially—and hideously—large-breasted women. (What a difference an "e" makes!) Silicon Valley, it turns out, was the place to be in the 1990s—the place to be, that is, if you wanted to participate in what has amounted to a second industrial revolution.

Physically, at least by California standards, there is nothing prepossessing about the Silicon Valley (roughly the greater San Jose area, south of San Francisco). Although California has never been noted for land-use planning, the tentacular spread of housing developments into the foothills of the Sierras continues unabated. And if the Silicon Valley is any indication, California has bought into the screw-you school of zoning so popular in Texas. Office parks in San Jose lie cheek-by-jowl with golf courses, strip malls, and, of course, more housing developments.

The overall effect is a kind of bland conformity, especially in the buildings that house these "revolutionary" corporations whose products have revamped America from Wall Street to Main Street. Indeed, bland conformity seems to be the point in this revenge-of-the-geeks America. In pursuing the holy grail of more and better and faster technology, we have become a nation of conformists. Our children—as well as more adults than I care to contemplate—seem content to while away their days engaged in some sort of electronic, mind-numbing violence. The wonders of the Internet appear to have supplanted the wonders of nature, even here in California, where nature in all of its glory awaits a couple of subdivisions away.

But for an increasing number of Americans it seems that the best approach to nature is mediated through a computer screen. The majesty of Yosemite or Yellowstone is only a couple of clicks away on the Internet—no waiting, no parking, no bears, no tourists. No interaction. A misanthrope's dream. I think the term is *virtual reality*.

During the course of my visit to the Silicon Valley I discovered an AM radio station devoted entirely to news about the Silicon Valley technology. The big news of the week was the visit of that Great Bear of the North, Bill Gates, whose arrival in San Jose was covered like a papal visitation. The radio station also runs reviews of new games and software programs. One began breathlessly: "This program has some really cool stuff!"

My purpose for visiting the Silicon Valley was to research an article on Thomas Kinkade, the enormously popular "painter of light." His soft-focus evocations of Victorian cottages and gazebos and sylvan landscapes have made him a very wealthy man. He appeals to some deep-seated nostalgia for a simpler past. Who can miss the irony that Kinkade's warehouse, where dozens of workers mass-produce, package, and ship reproductions of his paintings, is located here in the Silicon Valley?

But is it any wonder that a society barreling blindly into an uncertain future should want to connect with a past, even the mythical past conjured by Kinkade's halcyon images or by Knott's Berry Farm or Disney's Main Street, U.S.A. It is a sanitized, prettified past that we flock to see at Disneyland or, in the case of Kinkade's work, purchase in shopping malls: prints, calendars, greeting cards, Christmas tree villages, and, yes, screen savers for the computer.

After several days in the Silicon Valley, I had to get away; I couldn't bear another update on Gates's prophecies. I headed down toward the Monterrey Peninsula. Perhaps, I thought—I hoped—the benumbing, mass-produced conformity symbolized by the Silicon Valley was an aberration. For decades, after all, California has been in the vanguard of setting trends for the nation, even the world, in education, government, recreation, art, fashion, and cuisine.

My specific destination was Carmel, which I had remembered from a visit years before as a lovely village that, although lousy with tourists (like myself), had managed to retain its charm. And the underlying mission for my sojourn was the purchase of a small painting as a gift to celebrate my wife's tenure. Art galleries blanket Carmel—or, as the shopkeepers prefer, Carmel-by-the-Sea— and I must have visited all of them, hoping for an artist's interpretation of some tiny slice of California's majestic natural beauty. I found a few discrete California landscapes, tucked into back corners, but the hot items on the California art scene (if the galleries in Carmel provide any indication) are knockoffs of French Impressionism from a century ago.

Discouraged by the derivative character of so much I had seen, I headed down the hill to the beach. The cove at Carmel, framed by wind-gnarled trees and serenaded by the steady pulse of the waves, has been the subject of a million paintings and watercolors and postcards over the years. It is a place of unsurpassed beauty, and the breeze off the Pacific was sufficient on this crystalline afternoon to launch a half-dozen kites, their bright plumage etching curlicues in the sky. A few intrepid souls even braved the March waters.

It may have been my imagination, but even on this cloudless Saturday the beach was nearly empty, and the Californians who had gathered seemed almost indifferent—jaded—toward everything around them. Even paradise becomes monotonous, I suppose. As for the others, those who stayed away, perhaps they had chosen to surf the Internet instead of the waves, and they were even now doting on the flickering, electronic reproductions of the French Impressionists.

# EPILOGUE

I labour to possess my own soul.

Izaak Walton

# EULOGY

Clarence R. Balmer
February 3, 1929–February 24, 1997

---

To everything there is a season," the writer of Ecclesiastes tells us, "and a time to every purpose under the heaven. A time to be born, and a time to die; a time to plant, and a time to pluck up that which is planted."

Clarence Russel Balmer was born on a wintry day, February 3, 1929, in Columbus, Nebraska, just a few short months before the stock market crash and the onset of the Great Depression. Clarence was the sixth child and the third son born to Frederick and Lillie Balmer. His twin brother, Bernard, did not live to see the twins' first birthday. He fell to pneumonia and pleurisy and was laid to rest beneath the winter snows.

Clarence spent the springtime of his life working to scratch a living from the reluctant soil of southeastern Nebraska, a task made even more arduous when his father left to find work during the Depression—and never returned. Reinhold, his oldest brother,

133

enlisted in the navy. His sisters, Lillian, Esther, and Lorena, remained on the farm until marriage lured them away, leaving Clarence, his mother, and his grandfather.

The Balmer household could not afford a clock, so Clarence listened for the whistle of the Union Pacific as it passed by not far from the house; that was his signal to begin the walk to the one-room schoolhouse down the road. There he learned the "three Rs" as well as the beautiful penmanship that would adorn his correspondence throughout his life. He attended high school in nearby Monroe, where he graduated, as he recalled later, among the top ten—in a class of nine students.

Decades later, he would recount with boyish delight the day that Franklin Roosevelt's New Deal brought the wonders of electricity to the farmhouse. After the arrival of electricity, radio was not far behind. Soon, the sounds of music, comedy, and Mr. Roosevelt's "fireside chats" filled the farmhouse in the evening hours.

But it was Charles E. Fuller's *Old Fashioned Revival Hour* that really captured the teenager's attention and emboldened him to venture into Columbus together with his sister to attend a Sunday evening service of the newly opened Evangelical Free Church. "It was as though my entire life had prepared me for that moment," he said many years later. "I had tried and tried to get it right, but I always came up short." That evening he gave his life to Jesus. Within six months the Nebraska farm boy boarded a train for Chicago, where he studied for the ministry at Trinity Seminary and Bible College. He continued briefly at Wheaton Graduate School and earned the bachelor's degree from the University of Nebraska in 1957.

In the course of his studies Clarence met a remarkable young woman from the north side of Chicago, a woman of extraordinary beauty, grace, patience, and courage. He married Nancy Ruth Froberg on June 13, 1953, and over the ensuing forty-three years, eight months, and ten days they became lovers and partners—and the very best of friends.

To everything there is a season. . . . A time to be born. Randall was born in Chicago in 1954 during the seminary years, and four more sons coincided my father's first four pastorates: Kenneth in Lincoln, Nebraska, in 1956 while my father was an interim pastor in Phillips, Nebraska; David in 1960, while my father served in East Chain, Minnesota; Brian in 1966 in Bay City, Michigan; and Mark in 1970 here in Des Moines, where my father enjoyed the most productive and satisfying years of his ministry.

As he moved from the springtime to the summer of his life, my father's stories from boyhood served him well—the long walks to school, seeking shelter in the cornshocks from the winter wind, the low moan of the steam engine whistle in the distance as the Union Pacific thundered past the farmhouse on its way to the distant sea and then the black billow of smoke that hung over the tracks on cold winter mornings. He invoked the sweet taste of peaches from his mother's orchard, and his grandfather's insistence on straight furrows. Lock your eyes on a fencepost at the far end of the field, Grandpa Blaser admonished. Never look from side to side, and you will plow a straight line.

They don't make sermon illustrations any better than that, and for the young preacher coming into his prime the message was clear: Keep your eyes on Jesus; don't be distracted by the blandishments of wealth or fame or notoriety. Fix your eyes on Jesus, and your furrow will be straight.

For more than four decades Clarence Balmer lived by that maxim. A career that began in Phillips, Nebraska, took him as far east as Michigan and west to California, where he spent the final six years of active ministry as a district superintendent for the Evangelical Free Church of America. He served seventeen years on the denomination's board of directors, and in 1982 he was elected moderator of the Evangelical Free Church. He earned a reputation as a builder throughout his career. In Bay City, Michigan, he resuscitated a moribund construction project in 1964. Here in Des Moines he guided the relocation of the Highland Park Evangelical Free Church to this facility in 1970, and members of both the Bay City and the Highland Park congregations will remember that Pastor Balmer was always there at work on the new building—hammering nails, wielding a paintbrush, or installing a new door—night after night, working side by side with members of the congregation.

My father was tireless in those efforts; he genuinely enjoyed them. Sunday morning at the church in East Chain, for example, began with a twenty-mile trip to the nearest town for a live radio broadcast, then back to church to teach Sunday school and preach the morning sermon. After a sumptuous dinner at the home of a congregant, he might head back into town for a couple of hospital calls and slip in a short nap before returning to church to lead the youth group meeting and then preach another sermon for the Sunday evening service. No one loved his work more than my father, even in the committee meetings, which, by my reckoning, numbered somewhere in the range of four to five thousand over the course of a forty-year career. That statistic alone qualifies him for sainthood.

My father would be the last to claim this building or the building in Bay City, Michigan, or the addition in Freeport, Illinois, as a monument to him. A building, after all, even a church building, is merely brick and mortar. And if, for example, you mentioned the name Clarence Balmer to any of the fifteen thousand campers and staff members who pass through Spring Hill Camps in Evart, Michigan, every year, you will get a blank stare in return. Only a handful of people know that were it not for my father's leadership and determination the camp would not exist.

I suggest that if you searched for a monument to my father's life, you should look to the person beside you or perhaps into the mirror. As my father moved from the summer to the autumn of his life less than a year ago, the cards and the letters and the phone calls began to pour in, especially in recent weeks and months.

"Your father has had such an influence on me," has been the most common sentiment we have heard, "you'll never know." No, we'll never know, for among my father's many gifts was his determination to keep confidences. I suspect that he takes to his grave today the secrets of many of the people in this room.

"I just want to thank you for all the help you gave us when our daughter was pregnant," one woman wrote. "Your talks and prayers and strength made all the difference and helped us through many rough times." A missionary writes: "I want you to know that I owe much of my spiritual growth and encouragement to serve God to you, Pastor Balmer. You encouraged me, prayed for me, supported me, cared for me when my dad died. Through your ministry to me I have gone out and ministered to others." "I remember the time you came to see me in Monroe hospital," another letter said. "You made your congregation feel that you personally cared for them."

A huge basket at home overflows with such sentiments. "I have often told my loved ones about both of you," one letter reads, "Nancy's delicious bread and preserves and what a servant of the Lord Clarence was to so many." "When we resigned from the church it seemed that no one cared or noticed," a letter from California said. "Thank you for noticing." A card from Illinois: "I will always remember your visits when I had my pacemaker. You read passages from Isaiah. I still turn to them when I have fears." Another letter plucked from the basket: "After all this time I still miss you in our pulpit, Pastor Balmer. Our talks in your office helped me go on with my life in such a positive way. Thank you from the bottom of my heart."

"I remember Mom and her friends remarking how friendly and nice you and Nancy were to the 'old folks,'" another note reads. And still another: "I have thought so many times of the days I came to your office to share the pain and fear I had when my sister was battling cancer."

To everything there is a season. . . . A time to plant, and a time to pluck up that which is planted.

137

Someone else remembered the time my father cut short his vacation and arrived in the hospital room after midnight to offer his comfort, his touch, and his prayers. "You just don't forget something like that," he said.

No, you don't forget something like that.

To everything a season. . . . A time to be born. My father missed meeting his tenth grandchild by two days, but soon enough this newest grandson will hear stories about his grandfather. Someone will recall his passion for travel, his appreciation for natural beauty, the sense of wonder with which he approached the world. Few things delighted him more than a Midwestern thunderstorm, watching as the clouds rumbled closer and lightning creased the sky. Someone will explain my father's intimate connection to the land, how he never lost touch with his Nebraska roots. He dearly loved scratching the soil; it was by far his favorite form of relaxation to coax corn and tomatoes and roses and marigolds out of the loamy earth.

Someone else will tell of his infrequent but legendary loss of patience, which he usually worked through by pulling the vacuum cleaner from the closet and chasing it frantically around the house. Several people will tell the newest grandson about his grandfather's prayers. If it is possible to know God on a first-name basis, my father knew God on a first-name basis. His prayers betrayed an easy intimacy with the Almighty. He and his Creator were the best of friends.

Myself, I will probably tell this new grandchild about my own hospital encounter with my father a couple of years ago, when I lay suspended between life and death. For the better part of three decades my father and I had been locked in a kind of lover's quarrel over matters that seem rather silly in retrospect. When he learned of my illness he jumped on the plane to sit by my bedside day after day after day. That silent gesture was suffused with forgiveness and reconciliation, and I learned more about grace in those few days than I ever did from three years of seminary and a lifetime of sermons.

The new grandson, I think, will appreciate that story someday.

To everything a season. . . . A time to die. Clarence Russel Balmer died at home in his sleep in the early hours of Monday morning. He passed away in the presence of his five sons, a daughter-in-law, and his loving wife. His accounts were all settled—with his wife, with his children, with his God. He had run the race, and he was tired, and it was time to claim his reward.

The man who had given us life and who taught us how to live, it turns out, had summoned us for one final lesson: He taught us how to die.

It was an endless source of wonder to my father that a child of the Great Depression reared on the plains of Nebraska grew up to see the world. He traveled to most of the fifty states and to Europe, Asia, and the Middle East. But he had always wanted to see the fall foliage in New England. We arranged a visit to Vermont last October. The man who had reached the autumn of his life had come to watch the final, glorious explosion of color in the Green Mountains.

But his steps already had slowed, and it was clear by the end of the weekend that the brightest leaves had fallen. As my father headed home there was a faint scent of winter in the air. Winter was approaching quickly. Winter came too quickly.

To everything there is a season . . .

*Amen.*

# ACKNOWLEDGMENTS

S ome of these pieces have appeared in other venues, often in rather different forms: convocations, chapel addresses, church anniversaries, sermons. Several in the first section were delivered as the Staley Lectures at Houghton College, Westmont College, and Greenville College. Faculty members and students were kind enough to interact with these musings, and I notice as I write this that the one person I encountered at all three schools was James Mannoia, who has become a good friend. Earlier versions of other pieces were given at Wake Forest University, at the Princeton University Chapel, and as part of the Hugh T. H. Miller Lectures at Christian Theological Seminary. "Sins of the Fathers" was given in conjunction with the Cultural Life Lecture Series at Roberts Wesleyan College in the fall of 2000. On two occasions I had the honor of giving the Dotson M. Nelson Lectures at Samford University, where I benefitted enormously from the comments and the encouragement of students and faculty, especially James Barnette, minister to the university. "The Generation of Faith" also appeared in two anthologies: *Searching for Your Soul*, edited by

Katherine Kurs, and *The Best Christian Writing* 2000, edited by John Wilson. Several of the chapters in the second and third sections were syndicated columns I wrote for the *New York Times* News Service in the early part of the 1990s. Others appeared in a remarkable, now-defunct magazine called the *Reformed Journal;* still others appear here for the first time.

I am grateful to Rodney Clapp, Rebecca Cooper, and their colleagues at Brazos Press for their invaluable criticism and for shepherding this collection to publication. Barbara Lundblad and Robert Seaver of Union Theological Seminary have played the dual role of teachers and colleagues, and they have done so admirably. I also want to thank David Schlafer, Douglas Frank, and Sam Alvord for their guidance and especially for their friendship, which has now spanned more decades than any of us cares to tally.

Because this is in many ways a book about families, I would be remiss if I did not acknowledge the comfort, love, and solace my family has provided me. My life has been intertwined with my long-suffering mother and my brothers—Ken, David, Brian, and Mark—in ways that I can never fully comprehend, and I look forward to many more years of luxuriating in the tangled web of our relatedness. There are no words to describe my love for my sons, Christian and Andrew, and for my stepdaughter, Sara.

In a very real sense this book would not have been written—indeed, *could* not have been written—without the help of an extraordinary woman who has graced my life. Catharine is my lover and companion, my interlocutor and my best friend. Her sage comments on the various drafts of these essays are the least of her myriad contributions to my life. She has pushed me toward new levels of openness and honesty and candor. She taught me how to love. My father loved her dearly, and she, more than anyone else, is responsible for the reconciliation between my father and me.

I shall always be grateful for the numberless ways she has enriched my life.

# ABOUT THE AUTHOR

RANDALL BALMER is the Ann Whitney Olin Professor of American Religion at Barnard College, Columbia University. Born in Chicago in 1954, he has lived in ten different states and has held a variety of jobs, from haberdasher, house painter, and loading-dock worker to Congressional intern and magazine editor. He started his own small business, a janitorial service, at age sixteen.

Mr. Balmer has taught at Columbia since 1985, the year he earned the Ph.D. from Princeton University. In addition, he has been a visiting professor at Rutgers, Yale, Princeton, and Drew universities and at Union Theological Seminary, where he is also an adjunct professor of church history. He has written several books on American religious history, including *Mine Eyes Have Seen the Glory: A Journey into the Evangelical Subculture in America*, which was made into an award-winning, three-part series for PBS. Mr. Balmer was nominated for an Emmy for writing and hosting that series.

In addition to his scholarly activities, Mr. Balmer is editor-at-large for *Christianity Today*. His work has been published in *Sojourners* magazine, and his op-ed pieces have appeared in the *Des Moines*

*Register*, *New York Newsday*, *St. Louis Post-Dispatch*, and *New York Times*. Some of his writing has also been published in anthologies: *Searching for Your Soul*, *The Best Christian Writing* 2000, and the ninth edition of *The Norton Reader*. He has lectured in a variety of settings, including churches and colleges, the Smithsonian Associates, the New York Council for the Humanities, and the Chautauqua Institution.

Mr. Balmer and his wife, Catharine Randall, a professor of French and a scholar of sixteenth-century Calvinism, live in Ridgewood, New Jersey, and Stowe, Vermont.